THE STORY OF FIFTY YEARS

BY

CARRIE T. BURRITT

First Fruits Press
Wilmore, Kentucky
c2016

The Story of Fifty Years By Carrie T. Burritt, Edited by Emma L. Hogue

First Fruits Press, ©2016

Previously published by the Light and Life Press, [1935?].

ISBN: 9781621714934 (print) 9781621714941 (digital) 9781621714958 (kindle)

Digital version at http://place.asburyseminary.edu/freemethodistbooks/13/

First Fruits Press is a digital imprint of the Asbury Theological Seminary, B.L. Fisher Library. Asbury Theological Seminary is the legal owner of the material previously published by the Pentecostal Publishing Co. and reserves the right to release new editions of this material as well as new material produced by Asbury Theological Seminary. Its publications are available for noncommercial and educational uses, such as research, teaching and private study. First Fruits Press has licensed the digital version of this work under the Creative Commons Attribution Noncommercial 3.0 United States License. To view a copy of this license, visit http://creativecommons.org/licenses/by-nc/3.0/us/.

For all other uses, contact:

First Fruits Press
B.L. Fisher Library
Asbury Theological Seminary
204 N. Lexington Ave.
Wilmore, KY 40390
http://place.asburyseminary.edu/firstfruits

Burritt, Carrie T. (Carrie Turrell).

The story of fifty years / by Carrie T. Burritt ; edited by Emma L. Hogue.
213 pages; 21 cm.
Wilmore, Kentucky : First Fruits Press, ©2016.

Reprint. Previously published: Winona Lake, Indiana : Light and Life Press, [1935?].

ISBN: 9781621714934 (pbk.)

1. Free Methodist Church of North America--Missions--History. 2. Methodist Church--United States--Missions--History. 3. Missions--History. I. Title. II. Story of 50 years. III. Hogue, Emma L.

BV2550 .B83 2016

287.9

Cover design by Jonathan Ramsay

asburyseminary.edu
800.2ASBURY
204 North Lexington Avenue
Wilmore, Kentucky 40390

First Fruits
THE ACADEMIC OPEN PRESS OF ASBURY SEMINARY

First Fruits Press
The Academic Open Press of Asbury Theological Seminary
204 N. Lexington Ave., Wilmore, KY 40390
859-858-2236
first.fruits@asburyseminary.edu
asbury.to/firstfruits

THE STORY OF FIFTY YEARS

THE STORY OF FIFTY YEARS

By
CARRIE T. BURRITT

LIGHT AND LIFE PRESS
Winona Lake   -   Indiana

EDITED BY

EMMA L. HOGUE

DEDICATED

TO THE PIONEERS
OF THE PAST, THE DE-
VOTED LABORERS OF THE
PRESENT, AND THOSE
WHO SHALL FOL-
LOW IN THEIR
TRAIN

[8]

CONTENTS

CHAPTER   PAGE

  I   BEGINNINGS -   -   -   -   15

  II   PORTUGUESE EAST AFRICA   -   21

  III   SOUTH AFRICA   -   -   -   41

  IV   INDIA   -   -   -   -   65

  V   JAPAN   -   -   -   -   85

  VI   CHINA   -   -   -   -   103

  VII   DOMINICAN REPUBLIC   -   -   125

  VIII   HOME MISSIONS -   -   -   139
                  Panama and the Canal Zone
                  Kentucky Missions
                  Mexican Missions
                  Japanese Home Missions
                  Italian Mission
                  American Indians
                  Among Foreigners at Mason City
                  Greek-American Mission

  IX   WOMAN'S MISSIONARY SOCIETY   -   169
                  The Missionary Tidings
                  Missionary Publications
                  The Junior Society

  X   THE YOUNG PEOPLE'S MISSIONARY
               SOCIETY   -   -   -   189

ILLUSTRATIONS

Insert
Pages

Ellen Lois Roberts 16, 17
Mary E. Carpenter
Rev. Ernest F. Ward
W. M. S. Room, Chicago
G. Harry Agnew 32, 33
F. Grace Allen
Nellie Reed
Map of New Field in Africa 42
Rev. James S. Rice and Family 48, 49
Ebenezer Hospital
Portuguese East Africa Missionaries
Rev. J. W. Haley and Family
Louisa Ranf 64, 65
Yeotmal Church
India Map 66
India Missionaries 80, 81
Ethel E. Ward
Elizabeth Moreland
Ida M. Menter
Adella P. Carpenter
Helen I. Root
Map of Our Japan Mission Field 86
Rev. and Mrs. Teikich Kawabe 96, 97
Rev. and Mrs. T. Tsuchiyama and Family
Map of Mission Stations in China 104
Rev. H. H. Wagner and Family, Rev. F. F.
    Warren and Family 112, 113
Ruth Mylander, Gertrude Aylard, Lillian O.
    Pickens
Clara Leffingwell
Maud Edwards
Grinnell Memorial Hospital
Rev. E. P. Ashcraft

12 ILLUSTRATIONS

Insert
Pages

Rev. James H. Taylor
Map of the Dominican Republic 126
M. Grace Murray 128, 129
Edith Frances Jones and Lora
Rev. and Mrs. H. F. Johnson 144, 145
Rev. and Mrs. George W. Mills
Nellie M. Whiffen and Worker
Elizabeth O'Connor
Rev. and Mrs. Clyde J. Burnett
Rev. and Mrs. B. H. Pearson and Daughter . . 160, 161
Mary L. Coleman
Carrie T. Burritt
Emma Sellew Roberts 176, 177
Tressa R. Arnold
Rebecca E. Sellew
Ella L. MacGeary
Mary M. Robinson
Charlotte T. Bolles
Clara R. Freeland
Emma F. Shay
Ida C. Winget 192, 193
Edna C. McCarty
Evaline D. Green
Emma L. Hogue 208, 209
Lillian B. Griffith
Ella Maze Daniels
Lillian Camp Jensen
Alice E. Walls
Jenne Harroun Howland

[12]

INTRODUCTION

In this volume we have sought:

First—To show the expansion of Free Methodist missions in the separate fields in which the church has operated.

Second—To trace the growth of the various phases of the task—evangelism, education, medical work, industries and agriculture.

Third—To give praise and honor to Him who has blessed the efforts of all who have had a share in making this "Story" possible. For without the sacrifice, toil and prayers of many men and women in many lands there would be no story to tell.

The aim has not been to sketch the life of any missionary, or to give credit for all any one toiler in any department has accomplished. There is One who knows and never forgets.

We wish to thank all who have in any way assisted in this task; especially Miss Helen I. Root for information obtained from early files of the *Free Methodist;* also to Mrs. Emma L. Hogue for her untiring efforts in editing the manuscript and selecting cuts.

For all mistakes and omissions we beg your pardon.

CARRIE T. BURRITT.

CHAPTER I

BEGINNINGS

ELLEN LOIS ROBERTS

MARY E. CARPENTER

REV. ERNEST F. WARD

W. M. S. ROOM, CHICAGO

CHAPTER I

BEGINNINGS

FROM 1860-1880 the Free Methodist Church was absorbed in the effort to establish and extend its scope of operations in America. Little thought was given to the regions beyond.

However, in 1862 at the General Conference held in St. Charles, Illinois, a resolution was introduced and passed, providing for a committee to draft a Constitution for a missionary society. No report of this committee is recorded. At the General Conference of 1874, a General Missionary Board was elected. One of its duties was "to take charge of all the moneys raised for general mission purposes in the several annual conferences and appropriate the same to foreign missions or to the several annual conferences for home missions within their bounds as in their judgment the cause of God can best be promoted."

The General Conference of 1878 changed the powers and duties of this Board to some extent. The pastors were to hold missionary meetings and take offerings for missions, these sums to be for the support of missions within the bounds of the conference; but each conference might appropriate of its mission funds such sums as in its judgment it deemed proper, to the General Missionary Board. The term "Home Missions" at that time seemed equivalent to "Church Extension" of the present time.

At the General Conference held in 1882 at Burlington, Iowa, two advance steps were taken. Disciplinary provision was made for a General Missionary Board, also the secretary was no longer to be elected from the members of the Board, but was to be chosen by the General Conference. Vacancies were to be filled by the Executive Committee.

The following men composed the Board at that time: Rev. J. Travis, Rev. D. M. Sinclair, Rev. W. W. Kelley, Rev. J. G. Terrill, Rev. C. B. Ebey, Rev. T. B. Arnold, and Rev. D. W. Abrams.

During the next eight years, Rev. T. B. Arnold, the treasurer of the Board, by general agreement, corresponded with candidates, investigated their qualifications, and arranged for transportation—duties we now associate with the office of Missionary Secretary.

The Board was incorporated June 19, 1885. No missionaries had been sent out by the Board previous to that year. With that year begins our "Story of Fifty Years."

The following men have served as Missionary Secretary:

Rev. Charles Bond Ebey—1882-1890.
Rev. Walter W. Kelley—1890-1893.
Rev. Joseph G. Terrill—1893-1895—died.
Rev. Benjamin Winget—1895-1915.
Rev. John S. MacGeary—1915-1919.
Rev. William B. Olmstead—1919-1932.
Rev. Harry F. Johnson—1932-

In the early eighties, an appeal from "King Tappa" in Western Africa was printed in the *Free Methodist* which greatly stirred the church. His promises meant far less than they were supposed to mean. Many young people offered their services. Rev. and Mrs. A. D. Noyes and Miss Mary E. Carpenter were sent out as Board missionaries in September, 1885, to Liberia. They arrived on Thanksgiving Day. On Christmas Day Miss Carpenter was taken ill with African fever, and passed to her reward January 3, 1886. While her term of service was brief, her sister, Adella P. Carpenter, was privileged to serve for nearly forty years as a teacher in the A. M. Chesbrough Seminary. There she touched scores of lives who have done valiant service for the Master far and near around the globe.

In a few months Mr. and Mrs. Noyes returned to America and the attempt to start a mission in West Africa was abandoned.

CHAPTER II

PORTUGUESE EAST AFRICA

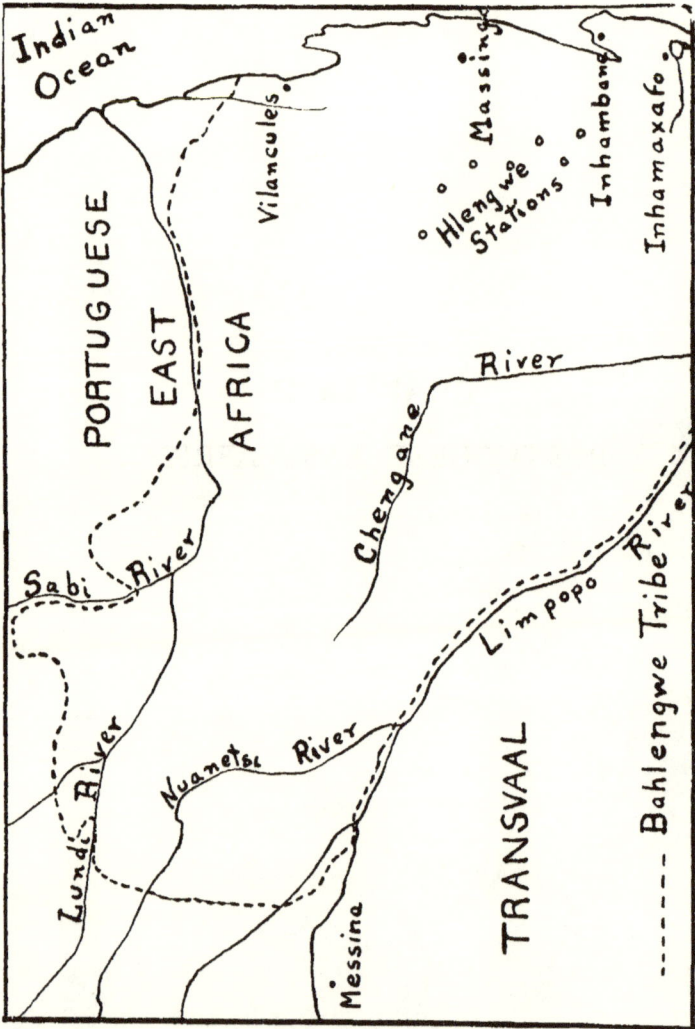

MAP OF OUR PORTUGUESE EAST AFRICA MISSION FIELD

Indian Ocean

PORTUGUESE

EAST

AFRICA

Vilanculos

Massinga

Hlengwe Stations

Inhambane

Inhamaxafo

Chengane River

Sabi River

Limpopo River

Lundi River

Nuanetsi River

Messina

TRANSVAAL

Bahlengwe Tribe

CHAPTER II

PORTUGUESE EAST AFRICA

(1885-1895)

	Began Service	Left	Died
G. Harry Agnew	April, 1885		1903
Walter W. Kelley	" "	1886	
Augusta Tullis Kelley	" "	"	
Robert R. Shemeld	" "	1893	
Katie Shemeld	" "	"	
J. D. Bennett	" 1888	1889	
Harriet Bennett	" "	"	
A. D. Lincoln	" "		1888
Abbie Lincoln	" "		"
J. J. Haviland	May, 1892		1897
Emma Hillmon (Haviland)	" "	1898	
Frank Desh	" "	"	
Rose Myers (Desh)	" "	"	

THE first missionaries to sail under appointment of the General Missionary Board went to Africa in the spring of 1885. They landed at Durban in June. Mr. and Mrs. Shemeld went inland and started a mission at Estcourt. The other three proceeded up the east coast and landed at Inhambane, June 17, 1885. A mission station was founded there and has continued until this day. Inhambane is in Portuguese East Africa or Mozambique.

Mr. and Mrs. Kelley, on account of failing health, returned to America the following year.

To the twenty-one-year-old Harry Agnew there
was no "give up." He remained in Africa four years
enduring great hardships. In the meantime he met
with an accident which permanently impaired the
sight of one eye.

In the spring of 1888, before Mr. Agnew's first
return to America, six new missionaries were sent
by the Board to Inhambane. Within a year all of
them were gone. Mrs. Lincoln and her infant child
died, then Mr. Lincoln a little later. Rev. and Mrs.
Richards of the American Board, hearing of the illness of Mr. Bennett and family, took them to their
station. Upon the advice of Mr. Agnew they labored
under that Board for nearly two years. Because of
continued fever attacks they returned to America in
1893.

The funds sent by the church in America were
insufficient. Our people at that time failed to com-
prehend the needs.

In the meantime, Mr. Agnew had spent a year and
a half in the homeland. While here he secured surgical treatment for his eye. Again he sailed for
Africa in July, 1890. This time after landing he
made the trip overland, walking some three hundred
miles to Inhambane. This gave him an understanding of conditions of life in the "bush" and offered
opportunities of telling through interpreters the
story of salvation.

In the spring of 1892 another party of four was
sent by the Board. In October Mr. Haviland and
Miss Hillmon were married. They remained at
Estcourt with Rev. and Mrs. Shemeld until the
property was sold.

Mr. Desh and Miss Myers were married in July, 1892. In November they went to Inhambane but their stay was short.

Again in 1894 Mr. Agnew visited America and attended the General Conference at Greenville, Illinois. Here he placed the needs of Africa before the church. A new interest and a better understanding of missions prevailed.

1895-1905

	Began Service	Left	Died
Susie Sherman Agnew	1895		1895
Lillie Smith Agnew	1897		
Carroll Smith	April, 1902		
Rosa D. Hunter (Smith)	" "		1932
J. W. Haley	" "		
Jules Ryff	February, 1904		
Lilla E. Ryff	" "		1920

After a few months Mr. Agnew returned to Africa. This time he stopped at Natal and in February, 1895, he was married to Miss Susie Sherman of the Vanguard Mission. They at once reopened the Inhambane work.

In June Mr. and Mrs. Haviland joined them. Then followed the opening of a new station at Mabili, a few miles distant. This station is situated on a ridge of land running parallel with the Bay, on the opposite side of which the town of Inhambane is located. The slope is dotted with cocoanut palm trees.

For many years the entire work centered around this spot. Sacred memories are associated with the mission house built by Mr. Haviland.

In December of the same year Mrs. Agnew, a bride of ten months, died of African fever. Heartbroken and ill, the labors of the preceding ten years seemed almost fruitless. About this time Mr. Agnew accepted the invitation of a Christian lawyer, Mr. A. W. Baker, to go to Johannesburg in view of engaging in a new type of work. In this section of Africa had been discovered the most productive gold mines in the world. Here were gathered laborers from all parts of the country and from India. The men lived in compounds. In their leisure hours, all sorts of vicious entertainments were available. Various missionary boards had embraced the opportunity of providing spiritual nourishment for the Christians, and of winning others to Christ. This seemed to Mr. Agnew a providential opportunity of helping the men from his loved Inhambane field.

The Board approved of this move, thinking the higher altitude would be more healthful for Mr. Agnew's impaired physical condition.

While all this was under consideration, Mr. Haviland died at Inhambane in March, 1897, on the eve of his departure for America. Mrs. Agnew and Mr. Haviland sleep in the near-by cemetery. A few days later Mrs. Haviland and the two children took ship for the United States. For some time as health and family cares would permit she traveled and spoke in the interests of foreign missions.

In May, 1897, Mr. Agnew was married to Miss Lillie Smith, who had been laboring in Natal as an independent missionary for three years. They soon went to Johannesburg. After permission was granted by the Board, a house and a schoolhouse were erected at Germiston, a short distance from Johannesburg.

In the spring of 1898, Rev. B. Winget, the Missionary Secretary, went to Africa, the first time a member of the Board had visited any of the mission fields. He remained nearly six months, supervising the interests of the work. The Johannesburg project was established on a firm basis. He was unable to reach Inhambane as no missionary was there at that time and conditions of travel made it unsafe.

For more than two years the Boer-English war hindered operations, and Mr. Agnew labored for a time in Natal and assisted in opening the new station of Itemba. Returning he found the mission intact and continued to supervise both the work at Johannesburg and Inhambane.

In 1902 Mr. Agnew, in company with Carroll Smith and J. W. Haley, the new arrivals sent by the Board, made a tour through the Inhambane country and was impressed with the fruitage from the seed so long planted. A church was organized at Mabili. This proved to be the turning-point of the work in this area.

Mr. Agnew had planned to bring his family to America in time to attend the General Conference, but as a result of fever he died suddenly March 9, 1903. He is buried at Germiston. His wife and two children—Susie and Harry—soon returned to America. Four years later they embarked for Africa.

How essential, though hidden, are the foundations of any structure. Years must pass before the wisdom of the faithful foundation-builders can be fully appreciated. This is emphatically true of the labors of the early missionaries in the East Africa country.

In March, 1903, Carroll Smith and Rosa D. Hunter were united in marriage, and at once assumed charge of the place at Johannesburg made vacant by the death of Mr. Agnew.

The missionaries soon learned to build on high ground. A second story for sleeping rooms was found imperative. Screened-in porches, boiled drinking water, and preventative doses of quinine have tended to reduce malaria.

1905-1915

	Began Service		Left	Died
Albert E. Haley	January,	1905		
Jennie Hamilton (Haley)	"	"		
Matilda Deyo (Haley)	Dec.,	1906		
Ethel A. Cook	November,	1907	1909	1925
Elbert H. Wells	January,	1911	1915	
Charlotte Johns Wells	"	"	"	
Ida B. Rice	"	1913	1921	

Early in 1905 J. W. Haley and Miss Hamilton were united in marriage. They labored in East Africa until their furlough in 1909, which was made necessary by the impaired health of Mr. Haley.

When Mr. and Mrs. Carroll Smith were transferred to Pondoland, the new arrivals—Mr. and Mrs. Ryff—took their place. Mrs. Ryff was born in England and Mr. Ryff in Switzerland. This gave them favor with the white people. After house-to-house visitation a Sunday-school was started early in 1906. There has been a steady increase in attendance and interest and it is self-supporting.

While in Africa in 1905, Bishop and Mrs. Sellew visited this part of the field where their ministry was much appreciated by our missionaries, and those of other boards as well.

Miss Ethel Cook spent most of her short term of fifteen months in the Inhambane country. She was considered a valuable missionary but ill health compelled her to return home.

In the summer of 1907, Mr. A. E. Haley and Miss Deyo were united in marriage. For a time they labored in South Africa, but since 1910 have been connected with the east country.

About this time the gift of a printing-press came as a surprise to the mission. It took ten men three days to roll it in a cylinder case the distance of five miles across the country. This has proved a great blessing. The Inhambane *Tidings,* so full of worthwhile news, is one of the products.

While Rev. J. S. MacGeary was Missionary Bishop, 1911-1915, he spent more than half of the time in Africa. He with Mrs. MacGeary gave special attention to the Portuguese East Africa area.

1915-1925

	Began Service	Left	Died
Ralph Jacobs	1915		
Ethel Jacobs	"		
Mae Armstrong	1917		
Ethel Davey (Ryff) March,	1918		
Lydia Ogren Gaudin, R. N.	1919		
Adelaide E. Latshaw	1920		

Ruth A. Moreland, R. N.		1923	1928
Gerald H. Bullock	February	"	1925
Rilla Thompson Bullock	"	"	"

After returning from furlough in 1912, Mr. and Mrs. Carroll Smith were assigned to the Inhambane field. Later Mrs. Smith wrote:

One of the most encouraging things we have to report is the large number of Christian marriages among our young people. Each marriage here by Christian rites means another Christian home.

In March, 1918, Rev. A. E. Haley and family returned to Africa, accompanied by Miss Ethel Davey. She had been a teacher, pastor and evangelist in Canada.

In the autumn of 1919, Miss Davey wrote:

I came to Germiston to learn Portuguese from Mr. Ryff, preparatory to my going to Inhambane.

Germiston is really a suburb of Johannesburg. It is 450 miles from Durban. Although it is now winter, Natal is still beautiful. It is the garden colony of the British Empire. Mr. Ryff has nearly forty native evangelists working under him. The natives pay their own evangelists and build their own churches.

In 1920 Mrs. Lilla E. Ryff left Africa for her heavenly home. Of her Mrs. Ella MacGeary says:

To know her was to love her. She was noted for her hospitality and her tactfulness with native helpers. She filled a large place with the white population and missionaries of other denominations.

Mrs. Ryff was buried at Germiston in the town cemetery. The plot is enclosed in blue granite curbing, and the stones are of the same, hand-polished. The stones for Mrs. Ryff and Mr. Agnew were gifts from the native church, the European Sunday-school and our missionaries.

From Inhambane Miss Armstrong wrote:

The pioneering necessary to opening up our work here has been accomplished. Now Mr. Jacobs plans to build the house for the single ladies. The materials are mostly on hand as a testimonial to his capability as a general manager.

The hot season is upon us in its full vigor. We think about the ice and snow you may be having. The spiritual part of the work is very encouraging.

In March, 1921, Mrs. Brodhead wrote:

We reached Pilgrim's Rest, in North Transvaal, on December 21, 1920. The work is truly wonderful in its possibilities. This is 300 miles from Germiston. The climate is splendid, the soil rich, the scenery beautiful. This Bush-buck Ridge area is densely populated by natives, and is the largest practically unoccupied district, so far as mission work is concerned, in all South Africa.

Mrs. Rosa H. Smith from Inhambane wrote as follows:

At our last quarterly meeting thirty-one babies and over a hundred adults were baptized; a large number of these were taken in as members in full connection and nearly a hundred on probation, and this notwithstanding the opposition from the Catholic Portuguese government.

In August, 1921, Mr. Brodhead wrote:

We are seeing real progress. We are buoyant with hope.

In January, 1922, from Inhambane Miss Nickel wrote:

This is a beautiful day. I hear the singing of the wedding party in the Christian kraal. A native Christian man and woman were just married at the church. They are singing the songs of Zion instead of old heathen chants. Our God lives and lives to conquer.

It became impossible to care for this growing work from one central station. A property was obtained about sixty miles southwest of Mabili. There are eight hundred and twenty acres in this tract with a river flowing through it. Natural resources are excellent. It is on the bank of a beautiful lake. There are fine garden spots, which help the food problem."

The project of erecting new buildings for this new station named Inhamaxafo was assigned to Mr. Jacobs. In January, 1922, he said:

We are putting the finishing touches on the pastor's house. The opportunities for gospel work here are unlimited. We are in the heart of heathendom. We need a doctor.

In February, 1922, Mrs. Jacobs writes from Inharrime:

We have had but little rain this summer. The people are facing the winter with no food and no money to buy it. It hurts me to see big men going to work carrying a native watermelon, a cocoanut, or a couple of ears of corn for their food during the day. Many times they go home and to bed without anything more to eat. I receive inspiration as I sing the song, "Pray on."

In May, 1922, Mr. Jacobs wrote:

I returned last week from a trip of ten days to our stations along the Inharrime River. I started from here in a boat which I made last hot season. I visited a station a day. It was a great improvement over traveling by donkey. About twenty of the thirty stations can be visited by water.

G. HARRY AGNEW

F. GRACE ALLEN

NELLIE A. REED

In May, 1922, Miss Reed wrote:

You will be surprised to see that I am off for Inhambane. I am well, so I see no reason why I should not go to help meet the need. With seventeen years of "seasoning" I ought to keep well.

In 1923 Mr. Ryff and Miss Davey were united in marriage.

It was during this decade that Miss Armstrong and Miss Latshaw each secured the "Secunda Grau," the second certificate that confers the right to conduct school anywhere in the province. This was a splendid achievement.

In 1923 Mr. Bullock wrote:

Almost one hundred per cent of these people are engaged in agricultural pursuits. Keeping the wolf from the door is fundamental in their lives, hence the need of teaching agricultural science. No other need is more pressing. A by-product of the gospel is better living conditions. We hope to place the work on a self-supporting basis.

Of this work Mr. Olmstead wrote:

There is no more fruitful mission field in the Free Methodist Church than Portuguese East Africa. The territory embraces nearly 5,000 square miles. Most of the country is wild and unsettled.

As related under "South Africa," this territory was at the annual conference of 1924 designated as Portuguese East Africa Conference.

In 1923, Mrs. Jacobs wrote of the results of the gospel at Inhamaxafo:

It is touching to see middle-aged men beginning with the primer to learn, and with a slate and pencil trying to write their names. It rejoices our hearts to see them so aroused from their lives of ease as to desire the better things.

After two years of service as nurse, Mrs. Gaudin returned to her home in Jamestown, New York.

1925-1935

	Began Service	Left	Died
Herbert G. Roushey	December, 1926		
Esther Landis Roushey	" "		
Lawrence Arksey	October, 1927		
Ruth Secord Arksey	" "		
Dr. Theodore Thomas	January, 1931		
Lois Adams Thomas	" "		

In April, 1925, the Portuguese East Africa Conference met for the first time after the division of the Africa work into two conferences. Mr. Ryff presided. His sermon Sunday was fittingly illustrated with word pictures true to native life. Later a native girl said:

I shall long remember the preacher's good words, because he told so many pictures.

All reports showed an increase in membership. Not a word of discord, but perfect harmony prevailed.

From Miss Armstrong:

Can you imagine our joy yesterday, as a witch doctor came with her whole outfit of charms, and knelt at the altar while Brother Jacobs was preaching. The work moves on.

Mrs. Rosa Smith said of the 1926 annual conference:

It is interesting to watch the intellectual as well as spiritual developments of the native Christians. The reports showed many problems but also victories. They are advancing on the line of self-support. Several large, well-built churches have been erected this year. A large increase in membership also was reported. The need of more workers is so great.

Concerning the Inhamaxafo School Mrs. Jacobs wrote:

Another term has just closed. The boys have not only made progress in their school work but many, if not all, have been definitely helped by the Lord. Miss Latshaw has reason to be proud of their progress. The Portuguese inspector gave a very encouraging report.

Of the annual conference in 1928, Mrs. Arksey wrote:

What a privilege to attend such a gathering! Brother Ryff presided with great acceptability. The appeals made on the conference floor brought tears to our eyes. Not one discouraging note. There is a splendid fellowship among the missionaries. On Sunday 1,500 people gathered under the trees for the services. The natives need no urging to testify. We enter the new year with renewed faith and courage.

From Mrs. A. E. Haley:

Our petitions have been heard and a car has been granted for this work.

In 1928, the Board authorized the purchase of an 800-acre farm at a low figure, sixty miles north of Mabili, in the Massinga territory. The location is quite ideal, the climate good. All this seemed to be answers to the prayers of the missionaries.

Rev. A. E. Haley wrote:

Our evangelists are a noble body of men. God bless them. When it comes to sacrifice, loyalty to the church and spirituality, I do not know where a body of men could be found that would pass at a higher rating.

Of the 1929 annual conference Mrs. Roushey wrote:

One of the most impressive things was the beautiful spirit in which the natives took all our decisions.

In March, 1930, Mr. Arksey wrote of the school at Inharrime:

Miss Latshaw is most capably manning the girls' school. She is filling a long-felt need in that she is preparing girls to become capable and intelligent Christian workers, wives and mothers. The new laws have not put us out of existence as they threatened to do.

In July, 1930, occurred the sudden death of Blanche, daughter of Rev. and Mrs. Carroll Smith. She was reared in Africa while her parents were serving the church on the mission field. Having completed her college course, she had made application to the Board offering her life service in behalf of the people of Africa.

Miss Armstrong in reporting the annual conference of 1930 said:

The reports showed sturdy strength and steady growth. The climax was reached when an immense crowd sat spellbound while the needs of their brothers away to the north and west were related vividly by our newly-ordained man, Sam Gudo. The Sunday morning offering represented an average yearly income of a Christian family in this land.

Miss Ruth Moreland, who had given a term of service as a successful nurse, came home on furlough and in 1930 was married to Mr. Albert D. Zimmerman.

In September, 1932, Mrs. Rosa Hunter Smith died in Los Angeles, California, where she had hoped to regain her health. She was buried in Tionesta, Pennsylvania. She was a tireless, capable worker, an excellent interpreter, a valiant warrior in her beloved Africa. Her life-partner, abundant in labors in Africa, now toils in the homeland as health will permit.

Concerning the annual conference of 1932, Mrs. Ryff wrote:

One improvement was the greater ability of the delegates in handling the business of the conference. Another was the good and intelligent testimonies the women were able to give. They had abandoned that crushed air that seemed to say, "Oh, we are nothing. It does not matter about us."

Late in 1932, Mrs. A. E. Haley wrote:

We received a hearty welcome home. The new house at Mabili is adorable. It is modern and airy, and not a rat or a bat to be seen anywhere. Where earth had been removed for road building we have planned a sunken garden.

Always in the background of my thinking while in America were the needs of the women and young people here. The response we receive when we try to have a Bible class or a women's meeting is most encouraging.

In 1929, three native pastors made a trip barefoot through burning sands, over sixty miles north into new territory. They found possibly 3,000,000 people untouched by the gospel. The Board in due time gave permission to purchase the land. For more than two years Miss Nellie Reed represented this new venture in her meetings in the homeland.

The plan of donating the price of one or more acres received great response.

From Mrs. Thomas:

It is an inspiration to know of the sacrifices made and the prayers offered for us. God truly has answered and given us the victory here in Lisbon. We passed our teachers' examinations and now Dr. Thomas has passed all nine groups of examinations at the medical school and will soon defend his thesis. We plan to sail for Africa, March 22. Our American-Portuguese baby, Clair Ann, will celebrate her first birthday at sea.

Again from Mrs. Thomas concerning the annual conference:

The fellowship of the conference meant so much to natives and missionaries alike that all were loath to leave. Inhamaxafo is truly a garden spot in this part of the world. Every one knew that their new doctor would be at the conference so brought their aches and pains. We are studying language lessons and learning to manage a house on a mission station.

In 1933, Mr. Arksey wrote:

The depression is proving a blessing in disguise. The small annual pittances of the native preachers have been reduced to almost the vanishing point. Self-support and spirituality have come to the front. The future for Inhambane under the benediction of the blessed Builder will be glorious. The church of tomorrow will be worth all we are able to invest in prayers, money and lives.

Again from Mrs. Thomas:

At the recent district meeting we were able to understand much of what was said. Fifteen babies and several adults were baptized. Nearly every one present consulted the doctor for one ill or another, real or imaginary, because they do love to take medicine.

From Dr. and Mrs. Thomas in the spring of 1934:

The three-years' course for nurses starts next week. Many do not even know how to read and write their own language, but they will be given practical training so they can go to the villages and care for the sick. Moral and religious requirements will be stressed.

Mrs. Ryff wrote:

Recently all the family visited one of our most distant points. Witbank is the center of a coal mining area. In the early days Mr. Ryff went there by train. Then came the motor car, God's boon to the tired missionary. Sometimes the roads are bad. Now we can go by car on good roads. The farms looked beautiful. Acre after acre of tall corn, sheep, goats and cattle grazing in the veldt, all made pretty pictures. We enter the cool church building feeling at home—our church—our people, won from heathenism. Thirteen joined the church. One of the number was a woman, the first to join our church here in the Transvaal.

Concerning the Massinga project Rev. A. E. Haley wrote:

With the application to do mission work we were required to submit plans of all the buildings that we expected to erect. Our applications received all the necessary stamps and vises, and the signature of the Governor-General. The first installment of money for the building is here, and we have gathered a very efficient staff of laborers. While we have much material on the spot, yet much has to be imported and transported from the port seventy-five miles distant. North of us stretches more than a thousand miles of territory unoccupied by Protestant missions. Has our church such another field as this? The first man to testify publicly to his acceptance of Christ is the chief-to-be, the nephew of the present chief, who is so opposed to the gospel coming into the territory.

To Mr. A. E. Haley and Mr. Jacobs we are indebted for the two wells in successful operation in the Massinga territory. To the natives it was a great miracle. Only the missionary's God could do such a deed. It was a great victory when sweet, sparkling water was found. The last fifty feet was bored through soapstone. The natives come for water in such crowds that they have to wait turns to get service. A great opportunity awaits the missionaries.

Concerning the 1934 session of conference Miss Armstrong said:

Two evangelists from widely-separated districts of this outlying territory reported their work in a heart-stirring way. The problems faced, the difficulties encountered, and the successes achieved made the conference feel the responsibility of meeting the cries for soul "help." Further self-denial and sacrifice on the part of the home church is the request.

1934 statistics show: Missionaries, 11; stations with resident missionaries, 4; outstations, 173; organized churches, 88; members in full connection, 1,917; members on probation, 336; Sunday-schools, 164; officers and members, 4,015; native contributions, $2,761.77; value of mission property, $41,-800.00.

CHAPTER III

SOUTH AFRICA

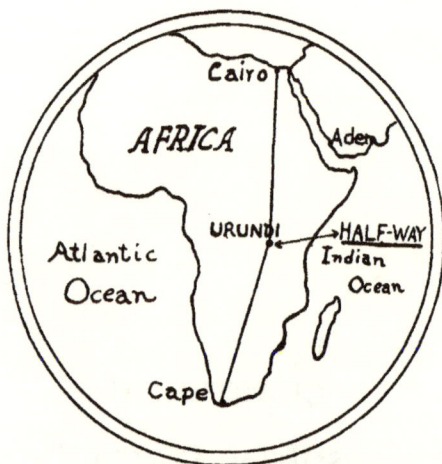

THE NEW FIELD IN AFRICA OPENED BY
REV. J. W. HALEY

CHAPTER III

SOUTH AFRICA

1885-1895

	Began Service	Left	Died
A. D. Noyes	November, 1887	1898	
Sophia Noyes	"	"	"
Ida Heffner (Spalding)	March, 1888	1893	
F. Grace Allen	"	"	

THE five missionaries sent to Africa in 1885 landed at Durban, but did not remain in South Africa. Of the six sent in 1888, the life work of only one is linked with South Africa.

Mr. and Mrs. Noyes labored for three years under the American Board, as needed funds were lacking on the part of the Free Methodist Board. However, in December, 1890, they began active work with our Board and continued for eight years.

Miss Heffner remained with the American Board for a time after our group was scattered by sickness and death. Throughout her life she was devoted to the cause of missions.

Miss Allen for lack of funds taught three years under the American Board, but never resigned from our Board. In 1891 she went to Fair View Mission Station and has continued in South Africa ever since. It was here she began her long career of teaching ministry.

[43]

Mr. Noyes went to Natal in quest of a mission field. At length he reached the Umzumbi River, seventy miles from Durban. The broad valley of fertile land seemed well-suited for a center from which to evangelize. It lies among the hills overlooking the Indian Ocean. The climate is mild, and the scenery beautiful.

Here in 1891 he purchased 2,265 acres of land at $2.44 per acre, with twenty years in which to pay for it, and no interest. Our Board bought this from Mr. Noyes. The plan was to let building sites to native tenants at five dollars a year.

The "hut rents" paid for the farm. With the development of the country, the farm increased in value many times the purchase price.

1895-1905

	Began Service		Left	Died
John Pearson Brodhead	April,	1898	1923	
Anna Sanford Brodhead	"	"	"	1929
Lucy A. Hartman	"	"		
W. C. Gray	"	1900	1903	
Willetta Gray	"	"	"	
Nathaniel B. Smith	"	1902	1905	
Martha Harris Smith	"	"	"	
Margaret A. Nickel	"	"	1934	
J. W. Haley	"	"		
Dr. W. A. Backenstoe	Nov.,	1903		1932
Mary Stillson Backenstoe	"	"		

In 1896 a new "wattle and daub" chapel was built to replace the round hut gone to decay.

In 1898 the Girls' Home School was opened by

Miss Allen. This proved to be a refuge for heathen girls who in order to serve the Lord must run away from their kraal homes. Later it became a standard Boarding School for Christian girls.

In 1898, after the departure of Mr. Noyes, Mr. Brodhead was made superintendent of the mission and pastor of the Fair View Church.

About that time a new Colonial law came into effect, that no public beer-drinks were allowed on a farm without the consent of the one in charge. This brought more desirable tenants to Fair View.

Also in this year the Sabbath-school was organized on the American plan. Heretofore the men, women and children were all in one class.

In 1899 the new Girls' Home School was built. The task of making the required bricks was a long and tedious one.

In that year a daily post-office was opened near Fair View. Previous to that time mail was brought from an office twelve miles distant once a week.

In 1899-1900 the boys of the Station School, under supervision, made good roads to connect with the Government Road. All this was a great improvement.

In 1900 the railway reached Umzumbi. This meant much not only to Fair View but to the "up-country" stations opened later.

The sewing classes at Fair View were of great value. The money obtained from sale of garments was spent for school furniture. Many of the girls were more skilful than white girls with their needles.

In 1902 a Compulsory School Law was enacted.

This greatly increased the enrolment, and the Government Grant as well.

In December, 1902, a wicked chief sent a messenger to the mission asking that prayer for rain be offered the next Sabbath day. An unusual number of heathen men were at the service. As the preacher began to pray at the close of the sermon, the big rain drops began to clatter upon the iron roof, so that his voice could hardly be heard. The interest became intense. The rain fell so heavily that it was difficult to hear the prayers and testimonies that followed. Several fell helpless under the convicting power of the Spirit. Many confessed their sins and prayed for pardon. The service continued for hours.

During the latter part of this decade several durable brick buildings were erected. One was a chapel to take the place of the "wattle and daub" one which was not expected to last over six years. The great problem in that undertaking was to transfer the bricks molded at the foot of the hill to the high ground. The native Christian women and girls gave great assistance in this task. Some carried ten large bricks at a time on top of their heads up that long hill.

1900-1901 marked the beginning of a new era in the South Africa field. In a marvelous way possession of Ebenezer station, also of Itemba and Edwaleni, was obtained.

Itemba is the second oldest station in Natal. There Miss Hartman, after spending two years at Ebenezer, went and entered upon her long period of teaching and evangelism. In 1904 a brick church was built. This was done without aid from the Board.

Edwaleni ("on the rock") is wild and romantic, yet beautiful and peaceful. It includes an area of over 1,000 acres.

It was here that Mr. and Mrs. Nathaniel Smith labored, but because of his failing health returned to America. He died many years ago. She, now Mrs. D. J. Santmier, is still interested in the cause of missions.

It was early in 1900 that the attention of the missionaries was called to Pondoland. This territory was set apart by the Cape Colony government for the exclusive use of the natives. No white men could buy land there. In the latter part of 1901 Mr. and Mrs. Brodhead and Miss Allen forded the Umtamouna river, though the current was swift and the bed of the river rocky. An influential chief, Patakili, invited them to open a mission among his thousands of subjects. After much delay a tract of thirty acres was obtained. There must be no delay in erecting required buildings. A near-by stone quarry proved a great help. A school, called Greenville in honor of our college in Illinois, was started there.

1905-1915

	Began Service	Left	Died
Nellie Reed	Jan., 1905		
Jennie Hamilton (Haley)	" "		
A. E. Haley	" "		
W. S. Woods	Dec. "	1926	
Annie Davis Woods	" "	"	

	Began Service	Left	Died
Matilda Deyo (Haley)	Dec.　1906		
Margaret La Barre	"　　"	1913	
Ole Kragerud	1907	1920	
George D. Schlosser	"　　"	*1908	
Newton Baxter Ghormley	Nov., 1907	1925	
Rachel J. Baird Ghormley	"　　"	"	
August M. Anderson	May, 1908		
Mary Damon Anderson	"　　"		
G. G. Kessel	"　　"	1917	
Hattie Flenniken Kessel	"　　"	"	
Luella Newton	"　　"	1916	
Elbert E. Wells	Jan., 1911	1915	
Charlotte Johns Wells	"　　"	"	
Ida B. Rice (Weaver)	1913	1921	

It was at the beginning of this decade that Miss Reed, supported by the Juniors, began her long career of teaching and evangelism.

Shortly after Miss Hamilton's arrival, she and J. W. Haley were united in marriage. On account of his impaired health, the family were obliged to return to America after four years of service.

In the spring of 1905 Bishop and Mrs. Sellew landed at Durban. The Christians and also many heathen had a share in the welcome. Seventy oxen decorated with palm branches hitched to one wagon drew the "Center Post Missionary and his wife" to Fair View Chapel. The scene was impressive. The missionaries sensed that a new epoch had come in their work.

The first Free Methodist Missionary Conference

---

*Transferred to China.

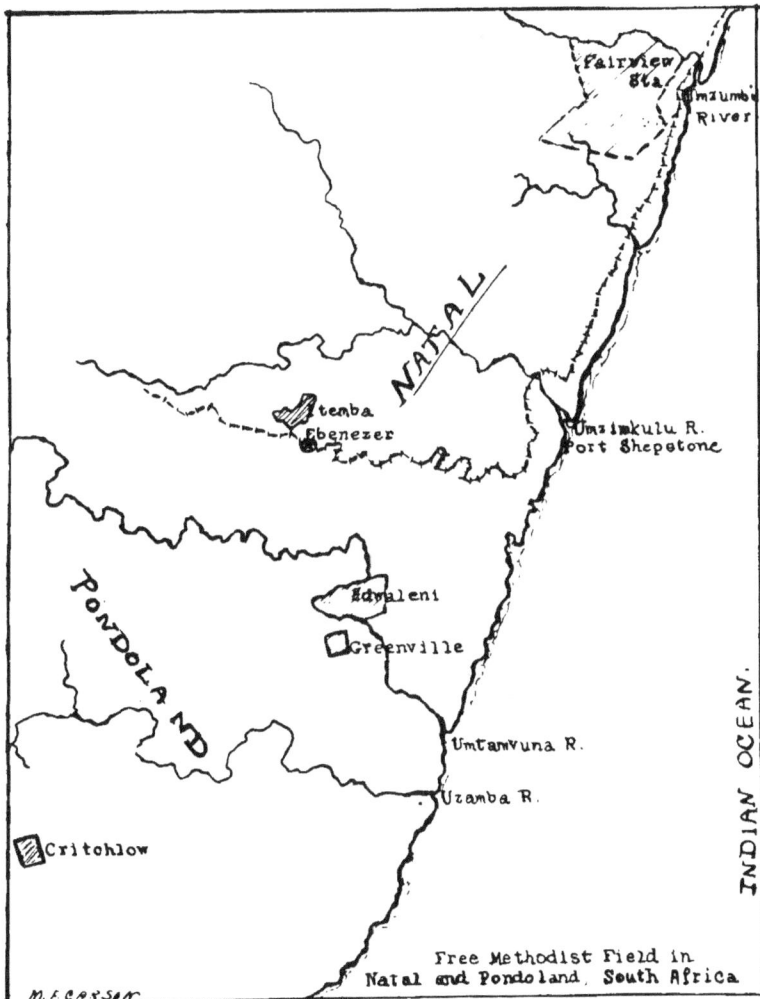

Fairview Sta.

Umzumbe River

NATAL

Temba
Ebenezer

Umzimkulu R.
Port Shepstone

PONDOLAND

Idwaleni

Greenville

Umtamvuna R.

Uzamba R.

INDIAN OCEAN

Critchlow

Free Methodist Field in
Natal and Pondoland, South Africa.

M.F.CARSON

REV. JAMES A. RICE AND FAMILY

EBENEZER HOSPITAL

PORTUGUESE EAST AFRICA MISSIONARIES

REV. J. W. HALEY AND FAMILY

was held in October, 1905, Bishop Sellew presiding. It was a wonderful time for missionaries and natives.

Mr. and Mrs. Woods soon after arriving took up their residence on the Fair View Farm. Twenty acres of bush land was cleared and planted with banana trees. Orange and lemon trees planted earlier were beginning to yield.

It was Miss Reed as Sunday-school superintendent who instituted the custom of giving a thank-offering from the gardens. Fifteen dollars was realized. The next year the amount was thirty dollars, and was sent to famine-stricken India. This custom has been observed each year since.

Miss Reed also organized the first W. C. T. U. among the women at Fair View, and the wife of Mpolosa Mqadi was the first president. This man was our first evangelist at Fair View. It was he who could remember every grave but one of 200 persons who had been buried there. The native people not having had books have wonderful memories.

Miss La Barre went out as a teacher. She assisted in the Boys' School at Edwaleni. Later she labored in Pondoland as an evangelist and was successful in establishing a permanent outstation.

After a term of service she returned to take a college course. At present she is toiling in the suburbs of Durban and at times assists our missionaries.

Mr. George Schlosser during his stay in Africa did faithful service in interesting the native young men in school work. He would take them out on the brink of a precipice and lift and roll larger stones than any of them could do. He told them his strength was not weakened by beer, tobacco, and heathen customs.

Miss Newton went out as a governess for Mr. and Mrs. Kessel's children, and later was accepted as a Board Missionary. Impaired health prevented her from serving more than one term.

Miss Allen writes:

In 1914 in answer to prayer, a revival broke out in the Girls' Home at Fair View. One night the Holy Spirit came in mighty power. Conviction seized upon the unsaved girls, and they could not sleep. One after another they came down and with tears and sobs confessed their sins, and found peace with God. The next day school duties were forgotten, and food was left untouched while the shouts of newborn souls mingled with the cries of the penitent. The results were deep and lasting.

Early in this decade Mrs. Agnew with her children returned to her chosen field and labored in South Africa until 1920, when she brought her son to America for his college and medical courses. The results of her labors still abide. Her heart is still in Africa, and her desire is to return, toil a while and die there.

1915-1925

	Began Service	Left	Died
James S. Rice	1915		
Mabel Kidney Rice	"		
Alice E. Evans (Hampp)	"	1922	
Gilbert A. Pine	1916	1921	
Virginia Parsons Pine	"	"	
William Caldwell	1919	1926	
Agnes Caldwell	"	"	

	Began Service	Left	Died
William S. Hoffman	August, 1919	1924	
Mildred Cady Hoffman	" "	"	
Daisy E. Frederick	1922		

In 1915 Rev. and Mrs. J. S. MacGeary returned to America in time for General Conference, at which time he was elected Missionary Secretary.

In November, 1917, Miss Allen writes:

We have been having the worst floods ever known in Natal. Many of the railroad bridges were washed away, and I could not get back from Durban. We get a post only occasionally through a native runner. The gardens are all washed away and we are threatened with a famine. The war still rages. Oh, what terrible times!

On January 1, 1918, Mrs. Anderson wrote from Pondoland:

Such rains have not been known in Africa for years. There has been much loss of life. Streams are dangerous to cross, thus making it difficult to get supplies.

In this same year the new church at Itemba was built. Men, women, and children had a share in this great undertaking. At last the long-anticipated Sunday morning arrived. Along the paths from the different hills the people wended their way. The dedicatory sermon was preached by Mr. Jacobs.

Concerning the thirteenth session of the South Africa Conference in 1918, Miss Armstrong wrote:

In spite of many hindrances and opposition, gains in membership, offerings, and kraal-visiting work were reported. The Edwaleni Training School and higher department of the Fair View Girls' School have been placed in the A grade, receiving highest money grants from the government.

In a letter from Mr. Woods in charge of the Fair View farm, he said:

The well is drilled and the water stands at seventy feet from the top, so we hope to have an abundant supply. The cost is heavy, but it is well worth the money, and the value of Fair View is enhanced by $1,000.

Our missionaries from the beginning had depended upon rain water caught in iron tanks during the rainy season for their water supply in their homes.

In the autumn Mrs. Rice wrote as follows:

We have had much sickness since May. Last week we started for Itemba in our donkey cart. The cart upset, tipping Lowell, our baby, Mabel Eleanor, and me out. The next day Dr. and Mrs. Backenstoe came along, also going to the district meeting. His horse became frightened and threw him off, breaking his collar bone. We are thankful that no one was killed.

Half of the boys of the school have had the "flu." It is spreading all over. Remember us in your prayers.

In a letter from A. M. Anderson early in 1919 he said:

In December we took seventeen into the church on probation, and two in full connection here at Greenville Mission Station. Twelve heathen were recently converted at Critchlow Mission Station.

Over 100,000 have died in South Africa of influenza, and the end is not yet.

Later in the year Mrs. Anderson writes us as follows:

The school here at Greenville moves right on. There are forty-six in attendance. The building apartments are kept neat and clean. The dining-room is large and airy. For three months the women joined with me in a sunrise prayer-meeting. Every woman at the ringing of the large bell left her task and went alone to pray. The teacher, girls and women who live near met in the chapel. This effort resulted in a marked increase in spiritual life.

In the autumn of 1919, Dr. and Mrs. Backenstoe wrote:

Ever since our arrival we have been looking toward Ebenezer as a site for our hospital. Ebenezer is four miles from Itemba, twelve miles from Edwaleni, eighteen miles from Greenville, forty miles from Fair View. It has ninety acres of land, with railway and highway passing through. There are perhaps 20,000 people within a radius of twenty miles, almost wholly without medical aid. Many of the missionaries who were sick last year had to go to Durban at expense to themselves and the Board. This shows the urgency of our need. One building, and that not a large one, is intended. We have a hospital on our hands whether or no. I wish you could see the well-traveled road to our house.

The wood-working and carpenter shop that is being erected is chiefly the child of the faith of Brother and Sister Rice, who are now on furlough. The building is 102 feet long, by 52 feet wide. The prospects are fine for the next term of school.

Early in 1921, Mrs. Anderson writing of the past year said:

A blessed memory. Disappointed? Yes. Discouragements? Yes, too many to mention. Perils? Yes, by fires, swollen streams, from heathen gossip. Sickness? Yes, flu, smallpox, and typhus not far distant. Loneliness? Yes, Pondoland missionaries must experience that quite often. Needs? Yes, a lot of them, spiritual and temporal. Hunger? No, the rains came, the gardens are fine.

We enter the new year trusting God and depending upon your prayers. We are thankful for the many cheerful letters received.

In Dr. Backenstoe's report at conference, 1921, he said he had traveled 1,500 miles the past year. Many of these miles had been on horseback, and oftentimes in the intense heat, sometimes in the night, when he could only trust his horse to find the path and cross the rocky stream. Sunday, March 13, was the doctor's fiftieth birthday anniversary. Young and old all contributed to assist him in celebrating it in a most fitting way. In May, 1921, Mr. Ghormley writes:

We are going along just like plow horses, up one furrow and down the next. Last Wednesday evening the Lord was pleased to manifest His presence unusually.

Our school is full and we are enlarging the room. When we came to this hut on the hill in 1908 we did not think of such developments.

In July, 1921, Miss Hartman wrote of visits to outstations:

The scenery was grand. We may miss many things in our isolated lives in this far-away land, but not many at home see the beauties of nature that we do. At one service an old white-haired grandmother was baptized and received in full connection. Maqumeni Cele, a naked herd boy, soon chose the Lord after entering Edwaleni Training School. Under Brother Rice's tuition he advanced rapidly. He passed the government examinations ahead of all competitors in the province. He won a bursary for a three-year course at Lovedale, but the rigorous climate caused his affliction of tuberculosis.

He died, November, 1921, aged twenty-one years. While life lasted he was a great comfort to the missionaries. He read many of the best books in Dr. Backenstoe's library. Another trophy was laid at the Master's feet from Edwaleni.

Mrs. Ghormley of Edwaleni Training School wrote:

The dedication service and district quarterly meeting was a most gracious occasion. We have been carrying a heavy load to get ready for the new term, but the glory that followed more than paid for it all. These buildings, these students, these grounds, these burdens, these victories are ours, but yours not less than ours.

Mr. Ghormley said:

The shop and the addition to the school are now completed. It seems too good to be true. Now each of the teachers has a separate classroom. We have nice clean dormitories for all the boys.

From Miss Hartman:

I believe the work is more encouraging here than in America. Recently I attended a Workers' Convention at Port Shepstone where I heard good holiness sermons. I very seldom hear a sermon in English to white people. I don't think I have heard ten in the last ten years, so it was a real feast to my soul.

Miss Alice E. Evans served as an acceptable teacher in the Fair View School, returning home at the end of seven years.

In reporting the South Africa Conference of 1922, Mrs. Rosa Smith said:

As we neared Itemba, some of us for the first time viewed the hospital on Ebenezer hill. How beautifully Miss Hartman all alone had provided for the comfort of so large a company.

The delegate of her circuit reported, "We have a man." God surely blesses and helps her year by year. At the close of the Sunday evening service the prayer and testimony meetings were characterized by "showers of blessing." The gain on the district after making good all losses was 200.

In September Mrs. Anderson wrote from Greenville:

In going horseback to Critchlow Mission Station we cross twelve streams of water. In some there are large, slime-covered rocks lying in the water in all sorts of positions. Our horses manage to step between or on top and slip off and flounder about until they get across. A short time ago we went to Durban. I had not been there in over a year. We went on our horses fifteen miles to the hospital. Dr. Backenstoe had invited us to leave our horses in his paddock. The train stops only a few steps from their door. They were expecting several patients soon. The building is roomy and comfortable.

Later Mrs. Anderson wrote of the Greenville Mission Station School:

Pondos are independent and careless, but intelligent and tenacious along lines of interest to them. Only when the Spirit of God shakes them tremendously do they yield to the light. Many of the girls thirst for learning. Here in the School they are taught how to sew, cook and wash and iron. Several of the girls are teaching in outstations. Some have married and their homes are better kept because of their training.

Again writing of the hospital, she said:

The hospital has been open now for nearly a year. It is a busy place. There is need of more furnishings. The rooms for the patients are cheery and airy. The verandas are so restful.

Miss Frederick in writing of Fair View School said:

After many years of delightful teaching in America, I find work here the crowning joy of my life. It is truly missionary work, for we live day and night in such close touch with these girls and so have a constant opportunity for sowing seed in receptive hearts.

An interesting item of business at the annual conference of 1924 was the division of the conference whereby the Transvaal and East Portuguese countries were separated from Natal and Cape Colony. This was thought to be for the general good of both sections and for conserving of funds. Rev. W. S. Hoffman was ordained elder.

In December, 1923, Miss Nickel wrote about the completion of the church building at Inhamaxafo station and the first service held there. Miss Nickel was working on the translation of Wesley's "Christian Perfection" into the native language:

Miss Hartman wrote:

A few days after conference I went to Etorjeni. We presented the matter of building a new chapel, as the old one was badly eaten by ants. After much talking it was decided to make brick. These people are splendid talkers and it is usually best to let them exercise their gifts, even though you know how it will turn out before they begin. So here we are hard at it, and have nearly half the number molded. We have good weather. One afternoon there was a heavy thunder-storm with much rain and hail. It came within two or three hundred yards of our brick yard. The people said Jehovah saved their brick. Do you think they were mistaken?

1925-1935

	Began Service	Left	Died
Frank E. Adamson	March, 1929		
Hazel Adamson	" "		
Ila Gunsolus	December "		

Mr. Rice of the Training School wrote:

The students are busy putting in gardens for the next term. Two crippled boys are making fine shoes. The white people order furniture. The head man of the kraal which Brother Olmstead visited when he met with us has become a Christian.

July, 1926, Miss Allen wrote:

When I think how the work at Fair View began among the children, and that those boys are now preaching the gospel, I am encouraged here. I am convinced now that God sent me to Pondoland, and I am content to be spent for the salvation of the Pondos.

In December, 1926, Mr. Rice said:

About 300 were present at the closing exercises of the school. Such a friendly spirit I never saw before among the neighboring heathen. One man said, "We used to refuse to let our people believe, but now we are consenting."

From Rev. J. W. Haley reporting the Fair View Girls' Home:

The government inspector gave an excellent report. The closing program consisted of fifty items. The walls were hung with well-made garments and beautiful needle-work made during the year. We heartily congratulate Miss Frederick on the year's work.

From Miss Allen, February, 1928:

Night came on and I was still miles away from home, with streams to cross. I could not see the path. The women were some distance ahead. I began to pray. All at once I was conscious of a strong man walking by my side. I did not see him with my natural eyes, but felt his presence. The horse went up and down the hills and through the streams until we reached home safely. Then my escort left me. Never before did I realize so tangibly the presence of the angel of the Lord.

In June, from Miss Allen:

Juba, our driver, needs a word of commendation. He took

seven loads over those hills, with no road, driving six oxen. Nothing was lost or broken, and no one hurt. Juba is a man of prayer.

Anna Sanford Brodhead died in March, 1929, at Los Angeles, California. More than twenty years had been spent on the mission field. To the last she retained her zeal and devotion for Africa.

In March, 1929, Miss Allen wrote:

I am busy getting ready for conference, which meets here at Greenville. The whole country seems to be expectant, and eagerly awaiting the meeting. Many of our Christians have built new mud huts.

In May, 1930, Miss Allen wrote from Greenville:

The first thing after my morning devotions I took my girls down to the brick yard and we turned over all the green bricks so they would dry well. I rode down and back on my pony. Then I went up to the home of our head teacher to bathe the tiny baby boy, and look after the mother. One of my industrial girls stays there all the time. We shall use this baby as a model to teach the girls and women the care of a child.

In September, 1930, Miss Hartman wrote:

I spent two days with Miss Allen in Pondoland. She is a soldier to take up a new line of work at her time of life and to live alone so far as white companionship is concerned. Yesterday was so cold no one came to the service. The people feel the cold very much, and they are too poor to buy the clothing they need. I am enjoying a nice fire in my fireplace.

From Miss Allen in the spring of 1931:

Many changes have taken place in my life since that eventful April morning, 1888, when our band of six adults and three children landed at Inhambane. Four of the number have gone to be with Jesus, and for many years I have been the only one of the party in this land. I lament many failures, but my covenant-keeping God has always been ready to pity and forgive. With Livingstone, I can say, "I never made a sacrifice."

From Rev. J. W. Haley:

On one of the farflung outposts on the extensive charge that has grown up during the thirty years Miss Hartman has labored at Itemba, a new chapel has been erected. Nkuntswana is situated on the flat-topped crest of a hill, between two rivers, in a land of wild grandeur.

The materials for the roof have been carried about ten miles up and down hills, on the heads of women. This, together with the plastering of the walls, represents a considerable free-will offering to the Lord.

In October, 1932, Rev. W. A. Backenstoe, M.D., passed beyond the earthly from Port Shepstone, South Africa. He was buried at Fair View in that lovely place overlooking the Indian Ocean. The missionaries were all present. There was an abundance of flowers. The stone that marks his grave was erected by contributions of the missionaries and his friends. It is a beautiful, black, South African granite, mounted on a block of white marble.

His ministry was faithful and fruitful. His cheerful and helpful disposition won for him many friends. He served faithfully twenty-eight years. The church lost an indefatigable worker in a land where workers are scarce.

In March, 1933, Miss Nickel at Edwaleni said:

Many women are seekers but still feel they must grind beer for their husbands. The women do much of the weeding. When they make a beer-drink and call the people to weed and drink, their gardens are usually very poorly weeded. The Lord comes very near. Oh, I praise Him!

In telling of a new church in the vicinity of Itemba, Miss Hartman wrote:

Seventeen years ago a sod chapel was built here, services were held, and a school carried on. This building became dilapidated and it was decided to build with brick. It was built by the people with no expense to the Board, thus teaching the people to do things for themselves. Men, women, and children all had a hand in the work. Brother Haley preached the dedicatory sermon. All this brings old memories of battles fought and victories won.

In January, 1934, Mr. and Mrs. Rice and family went "home" to their Edwaleni School, South Africa. Twenty years ago they first went to that land. Their return was providentially secured through prayer.

The kerosene lamps were very inadequate for lighting the large chapel and rooms of students. Before leaving America, a fine lighting plant was given to the Rice family for this purpose. The day the conference opened, the switch was turned on and for the first time at Edwaleni electric lights shone out from the chapel. The lights are several miles over the hills.

From a recent letter from Miss Allen we quote:

At last in His gracious providence I am back at Fair View, dwelling among my own people as I call them. I have seen these natives grow from infancy to gray-haired men and women. They gave me a hearty welcome.

The Bible School opened August 13. Thus far there are two classes for men and two for women, one in Zulu and one in English.

The W. M. S. are interested in the work and promise to help with the gardens.

Having seen the advance made in the past thirty

years by the native church in evangelism, trades, agriculture and self-support, J. W. Haley in 1923 became burdened with the thought that it was time to go to other parts of Africa where the gospel had not been heard.

After much inquiry he was directed to Urundi, in the Belgian Congo country. In 1926 the Missionary Board decided to enter that field, but on account of financial conditions the matter has been delayed from year to year. This "waiting time" has been very hard for our missionary.

The investigating trip some two years ago led through Natal, the Transvaal, Southern and Northern Rhodesia, and on into the Congo territory eighty miles north of Elizabethville. The grandeur of the mountains and the magnificence of Victoria Falls were viewed en route. At length Lake Tangangike was reached, then later by steamer on to Urundi. The country rises 7,000 feet above sea level and forms the watershed between the Nile and Congo systems. Although only about four degrees south latitude, its climate is temperate. Oranges, bananas, peaches, strawberries, potatoes, wheat and coffee thrive.

In the evening pillars of smoke from the mountainsides reveal the presence of people and forms a mute appeal to heaven.

Government requirements have caused many delays. At last on November 26, Brother Haley, his passport having been vised, started on the long journey to seek the realization of his cherished plans. The family will remain in South Africa until the mission is established and recognized by the Belgian government. Much prayer needs to be offered in behalf of this project.

ASSOCIATE MISSIONARIES

Mr. and Mrs. A. A. Miller, Harriet Sheldon (Barnes), Miss Myrta Smith, Miss Maud Creters.

1934 statistics show: Missionaries, 13; stations with resident missionaries, 5; outstations, 37; organized churches, 13; members in full connection, 645; members on probation, 456; Sunday-schools, 24; officers and members, 854; native contributions, $1,211.12; value of mission property, $136,100.00.

LOUISA RANF

NFORMAL CHURCH

CHAPTER IV

INDIA

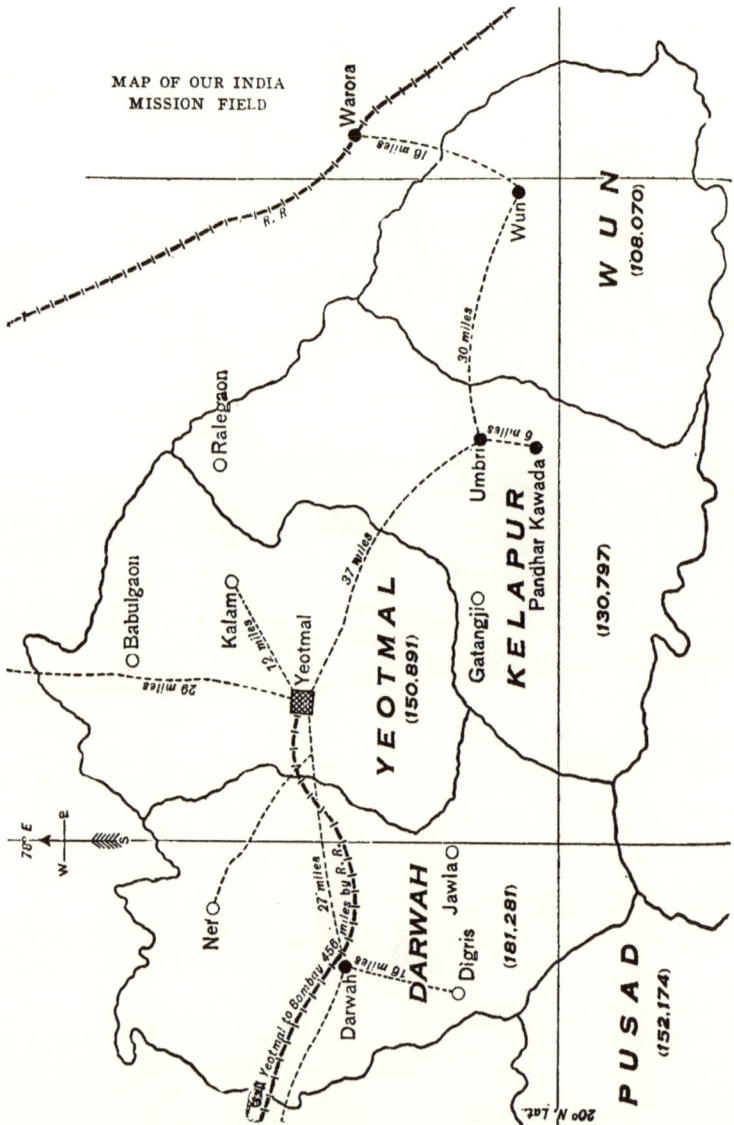

MAP OF OUR INDIA
MISSION FIELD

CHAPTER IV

INDIA

1885-1895

	Began Service	Left	Died
Ernest F. Ward	December, 1880	1927	
Phoebe Cox Ward	" "		1910
M. Louisa Ranf	" 1885		1890
Julia Zimmerman	" "	1886	
Celia J. Ferries	February, 1891	1903	
Anna Jones	August, 1892	1897	
Mattie J. Miller	November, 1894	1900	

WHILE the Illinois Conference was in session in 1880 at Freeport, Illinois, an unusual event took place. Ernest F. Ward announced to the conference that he and his wife were called to India and were going soon. They did not offer themselves to the organized Board that already existed. They did not ask its support. They did want the authorization and prayers of the church.

The conference was deeply touched. Mr. Ward was ordained deacon and elder by the general superintendent, Rev. E. P. Hart. The conference appointed him to labor as a missionary in northern central India.

This man and his wife paid their own way to India with money the wife had saved. They went out

---

Mr. and Mrs. Ward went out independently.

as faith missionaries, but they went with the con-
fidence and prayers of the church, and for some
years were listed among "Our Missionaries" in the
Free Methodist. The editor received and sent funds
as gifts from our people.

Rev. S. K. J. Chesbro gave the first printed sug-
gestion of aiding in their support. In December,
1880, while they were enroute to India he proposed
that each Sunday-school should take at least four
offerings for this work. The editor of the *Free
Methodist* said: "We endorse the plan; let the Sunday-schools support the mission in India."

In March, 1882, Rev. B. T. Roberts in the church
paper said: "We are glad so many of our pastors
are taking collections for Brother and Sister Ward."

They labored first at Burhanpur. Later for several years they were at Ellichpur, Central India.

While here Miss Ranf shared their toils during
her five years on the field. Her tragic death, caused
by the explosion of a kerosene lamp, was lamented
by Hindus and Mohammedans as well as Christians.
Sacrifice and devotion marked her daily life.

Soon after Miss Ferries arrived, she spied out the
land in the Province of Berar and had decided that
Yeotmal was a suitable place in which to begin the
work of Free Methodist Missions in India. After
the arrival of Miss Jones, the two women rented a
house and began to tell the gospel story. A year later,
in 1893, a bungalow was built.

Yeotmal has proved to be a very desirable center
for our missionary work in India. From here the
missionaries have gone out in different directions
and opened several very promising stations.

1895-1905

	Began Service	Left	Died
Emma Appling	October, 1896	1907	1913
Horace L. Crockett	" 1897	1900	
Abbie Crockett	" "	"	
V. G. McMurry	" "	1903	
J. T. Taylor	January, 1901	1919	
Margaret Fallon Taylor	" "		1919
Effie Southworth	" "	1913	
Rose Cox	" "	1913	
Mortimer C. Clarke	September, 1901	1908	
Ethel Helm Clarke	" "	"	
Mary E. Chynoweth, R. N.	Jan., 1902		1908

The little band of three that remained on the field found themselves face to face with the problems of a famine crisis.

In 1897 the transfer to the "big bungalow" with its twenty-five acres of land was made.

It was here that temporary quarters were set up for the girls, and a place for the boys on the land formerly purchased. Thus the orphanage work was launched and later permanent buildings were erected.

In the summer Mr. McMurray and Miss Ferries were united in marriage.

In a letter from Rev. H. L. Crockett we quote:

Six months ago we gathered our first sheaf of the coming harvest as a wave offering before the Lord. Nine orphan boys and eight girls have been baptized. It was an impressive Marathi service and full of promise for the future.

A new station was opened at Wun, sixty-seven miles southeast of Yeotmal. This was formerly the capital of the district and the center of Hinduism. In 1902 a stone bungalow under the supervision of Mr. McMurry was erected. Mr. and Mrs. Taylor and Miss Cox moved into this.

Mr. Clarke, in writing of their first Christmas in India, said:

As the light of day was beginning to dawn, we were awakened by the most beautiful carols sung by some of the orphan boys who had crept noiselessly up on the veranda. What a blessing it brought to all our hearts! Later the children all sat under a large tree, and after a few appropriate remarks by one of the native preachers and prayer, the gifts were given out. We shall never forget the looks of surprise and happiness on their faces. This was a red-letter day in their lives.

1905-1915

	Began Service	Left	Died
The Ward Family	1906		
Samuel D. Casberg	January, 1906	1929	
G. G. Edwards	" "	1911	
Grace Smith Edwards	" "	"	
Gertrude Alcorn	October 1906		
Jessie Lively	December "	1929	
Mata D. Alee	November, 1907		
Edith M. Santee	" "		
Herbert M. Damon	" 1909	1918	1924
Edna Sherman Damon	" "		
Louise D. Calkins	" "		
Frederick G. Mynett	October "	1913	
Abraham A. Lind	March 1910		
Ella Becker (Cochrane)	Oct., 1913	1916	
Elizabeth Moreland	" "		
Lorena Marston, R. N.	" "		1916
Clyde C. Foreman	" "	1914	

Frances M. Foreman   October   1913   1914
Elizabeth Tucker Ward   1914   1915
Effie G. Cowherd   "   1914   1921

During the cool season of 1905 there was a mighty outpouring of the Spirit on our district as well as other parts of India. The revival that followed will ever be remembered by those who were privileged to witness it. The results still abide.

In 1906 a station was opened at Darwha, twenty-seven miles west of Yeotmal. Here a mile from town E. F. Ward and wife pitched the mission tent and began work. Outbuildings, including wood house and cook house, were first erected and used for living quarters while the bungalow was being built. This is on a rise of ground overlooking the village. The building is light, airy, pleasant and convenient.

In 1908 Mrs. Ward wrote:

As I sit in my easy chair these hot days sewing, enjoying a shelter from the burning heat, my mind goes back to the last two seasons, when I was out at all hours of the day, helping to look after the workmen. The hot winds almost blow a gale sometimes, but we enjoy the coolness inside the bungalow.

I am getting better acquainted with the women, and often get invitations to come inside. I get their attention at once when I say, "I am the mother of three girls." That touches their hearts. They are sorry because I have no son.

Mrs. Ward's home-going came in 1910, just three months after reaching America. She is buried in the beautiful cemetery on Queen Ann's Hill in Seattle.

The death angel for the first time visited the mission in January, 1908, and took the much-loved nurse and evangelist, Miss Chynoweth. Her illness was a violent case of smallpox.

In 1908 Mr. Casberg and Miss Lively were united in marriage.

During this year, on account of the wife's impaired health, Mr. and Mrs. Clarke returned to America. Mr. Clarke's principal work was in connection with the Boys' Orphanage. The industrial work that he introduced was so successful that it attracted wide attention.

After long delays, eighteen acres of land were purchased at Umbri in 1909. This is a small village midway between Yeotmal and Wun. Mr. and Mrs. Casberg were stationed there and erected mission buildings. The bungalow is a stone structure from stone quarried on the near-by land. It overlooks a beautiful stretch of farming country. The government road passes the bungalow.

Landour, situated on the foothills of the Himalayas, over 6,000 feet above sea level, is one of the most beautiful places in India. Hundreds of native shops in the bazaar and a few European establishments supply nearly everything that is needed. In the hot season hundreds of missionaries go there for a few weeks at least. There is a language school, and other schools for European and Anglo-Indian children and young people. All these are successfully carried on by missions.

Chynoweth Rest Home is a life-saver to our India missionaries. Here they receive inspiration and spiritual uplift from mingling with missionaries of other denominations. This property was acquired in 1913.

1915-1925

	Began Service	Left	Died
Grace Barnes	1916		1918
Helen I. Root	1917	1922	
Rolland N. Davis	1919		
Melba Smith Davis	"		
Winfred Thuline	"	1932	
Evangeline Crockett (Thuline)	"	"	
Floyd Puffer	1920		
Edna Puffer	"		
Persis Phelps, R. N.	1922		
Ida Menter, R. N.	"		
Elmer S. Root	1923		
Loretta P. Root	"		

Again death entered the fold in 1916. This time Miss Marston, the nurse, was taken by smallpox.

For fifteen years the missionaries and Indian Christians had saved their self-denial money to build a new church at Yeotmal. One of the orphan boys made all the benches. The first service was held in January, 1916. Brother Ward preached the first sermon. His text was: "I will dwell in them."

Since that time there have been many meetings held there—weddings, funerals, welcome and farewell gatherings, also revival meetings where scores have found the Lord.

From Miss Root in 1918:

Yeotmal, a place of prayer, toil and many hopes! A place of tremendous possibilities for the Kingdom. We have a fine property with room for expansion. No famines in late years, hence few orphans needing homes. May the day soon come when we shall see the mighty power of God displayed throughout this beautiful field which has been given to us to cultivate.

In a letter from Miss Calkins, she said:

We visit all the bazaars we can, do all the calling we can when the mud is not too deep, and visit the women once a week in the large village where we get our mail and supplies. India needs the united help of all her friends. A long pull, a strong pull, and a pull all together, in pulpit, press and platform; but most of all at the mercy-seat.

In a letter from Miss Ward we quote:

I am getting acquainted with the government school children also, and am thoroughly interested in my "parish." I hope to call on every family in Wun if possible.

Again from Miss Barnes:

We all knew it would be the last quarterly meeting held by our superintendent, Rev. J. T. Taylor, as the condition of his wife's health demands their immediate return to America. We missionaries come and go—but the work must go on forever! Ah, sometimes it looks as if the work here is going slowly, but oh, friends at home, *the cross is winning its way.*

On October 19 of the same year the author of the above words finished her life's work following an attack of influenza. All her years at home were spent in getting ready for her two years of service in India. She passed the two-years' course in Marathi (language) in nine months. She was so happy in her Sunday-school work and also in the bazaar and street meetings. "God moves in a mysterious way." In "An Alabaster Box" Miss Root tells Miss Barnes' life story.

In a personal letter, 1919, Miss Root said:

I have been to Bombay to take my second examination,

to shop for the school, and finally to take a wee vacation. I stayed at the Missionary Rest Home. Returning I found the little handful of missionaries hard, hard at work. Tradition says we must have our bungalows whitewashed in November, and this year because of so much sickness it seemed unusually necessary. They were all tired out.

At the India W. C. T. U. Convention at Lucknow in the fall of 1919, Miss Root was chosen national superintendent of the Juvenile department. Her experience in similar activities in New York State served her well.

Again from Miss Root:

Great changes are taking place in the thought of the people, and even a year makes a very great difference in their attitude towards us and our message. Yet, how puzzling it all is. Often something occurs to turn them away from us and we are continually being baffled.

Late in 1919, Miss Southworth wrote:

In India diseases abound. Ignorance and superstition unfit the people to cope with it. For years your missionaries here have been pleading for a hospital. When we learned China was to have a hospital, we rejoiced. Our hearts were gladdened when we learned that Africa, too, was to have a hospital with Dr. Backenstoe at its head. At its recent meeting the Board undertook the task. Will the money be forthcoming?

Mrs. J. T. Taylor, having suffered many months, died in Hermon, California, December 18, 1919. Of her Miss Southworth says:

She had an attractive personality. Europeans and Indians all liked her. In each orphanage she won the hearts of the children. She always had time for everybody. Many a poor, troubled heart fled to her. Many a time Satan's hosts withdrew and the floodgates of heaven opened as she wrestled with God.

In 1920 Mrs. Casberg of Umbri wrote:

The foundations for both the hospital and girls' orphanage are dug, 40,000 bricks are burned, and more in the kiln, and the sand is mostly hauled. The foundations are to be built of stone and the walls of brick. No lumber can be obtained until July.

In October, 1920, Mrs. Davis wrote:

The crops are drying up in the fields. The people are rushing to the jungles for grass, so we must go, too, before it is all gone. The well for the bungalow is dry, and the one at the girls' orphanage is low.

In November, 1920, Miss Alcorn wrote:

We are having such a water famine as India has hardly ever seen. There is great suffering for both man and beast. The crops, too, were almost a failure.

In November, 1921, from Mrs. Casberg:

Some were surprised that the missionaries unanimously chose Umbri for our medical work. The village itself is very insignificant, but it is on the government road between Yeotmal and Wun. It is in the midst of a thickly-settled region. There is no medical help for miles around. Medicine was given out last year to 3,406 people, and the number is increasing.

On Thanksgiving day, 1921, Winfred N. Thuline and Evangeline Crockett were married.

In the spring of 1922, the new orphanage for the girls at Umbri was completed. "Moving day" was a great event. To be taken into a town they had never seen, into a new building and in an automobile, was a strange experience.

In February, 1922, Mrs. Thuline said:

We are really in Umbri. The buildings are fine and the children seem to be happy. The people from the villages all around are interested in everything on the compound. A family of a dozen nursery children is quite a responsibility to assume all at once, but I enjoy the work. Every missionary on this field needs your prayers.

In writing of the hospital building, Mr. Casberg says:

I never saw such a building drive as now; good masons are at a premium. I must burn my own lime and get the roof timber out of the jungles, fourteen miles away. Workmen are hard drinkers and many fail to appear on Monday.

Brother Ward in writing of an April windstorm said that eight sheets of ten-foot corrugated roofing from buildings on the Darwha Mission Station went flying through the backyard. That not even the stock were injured, he said, was a miracle.

From a letter from Miss Ward we quote:

There are so many reminders here at Darwha of my precious mother. It seems as though I am really carrying on her work. The only thing hard to understand is why my darling Louise wasn't spared to do her share, too, for she was far more talented than I; but "some day we'll know why clouds instead of sun were over many a cherished plan." Our India work was never more encouraging than now. I could write a whole page about the new missionaries sent out two years ago. They have all done well in the language.

Where can you find a better showing than among the orphanage children, and then think of their parentage! And how promising the grandchildren are. Over forty of our old boys and girls are in mission employ.

We had copious rains last rainy season, and there is plenty of water in all our wells.

Miss Helen I. Root, who found it impossible to remain in India on account of the climatic conditions, was a delegate from India to the World's W.

C. T. U. Convention in Philadelphia, in November, 1922.

Mrs. Minnie Johnson of Southern California, after visiting the schools of the India mission, said:

Comparing the work in India with other mission fields, it is evident that in this field the children are the hope of the church. Many of the Christian communities in India have been built up by natives who were reared from childhood in the orphanages.

In 1923 Mrs. Casberg concerning the hospital wrote:

Our hospital is almost ready for use. The government civil surgeon from Yeotmal is highly pleased with it. The medical work is one of the best agents there is for preparing the way for the gospel. I believe that the Great Physician Himself is going to constitute one of our staff.

Rolland Davis in writing of the Bible School said:

The purpose is to give to the Indian preachers and Bible women as thoroughly as possible a working knowledge of the Bible. This is done by direct study of the Bible itself, also such studies as theology, church history, evangelistic methods and Indian religions. The aim is to induce continued habits of study. Much practice work is accomplished. Fourteen Sunday-schools are carried on.

Brother Ward in reporting a year's work said:

I preached 225 times in seventy-six towns and villages; visited two religious fairs and several railroad trains; 700 gospels and booklets were sold; 500 leaflets given out.

1925-1935

From Miss Moreland:

One of our new ways of working is with the motorcycle, the gift of the children of the southland. We are getting more and more experienced in driving on the country roads. The cycle and side car are narrow enough to run in the cart ruts. Of course it is no trouble to get a crowd as soon as the "put-put-ee" arrives.

From Miss Cowherd:

The Christmas program in the Girls' School was perfectly splendid. The girls arranged it themselves, even the decorations. Afterwards they came into our part of the house, where we had loaded a tree with their gifts. The girls take turns in cooking, about a dozen at one time.

From Miss Menter:

How ignorant the people seem to be about caring for their health. Our efforts in helping sick bodies are all put forth so that precious souls may be saved.

From Miss Ward:

We were just thinking about the song, "December's as pleasant as May." That is more than true here, for December in India is delightful weather. But May! Whew! The hot winds, baked earth, dust, ants, flies and the sun's rays! But we are finding May pleasant. We think some one or ones are praying for us.

As a Christmas gift from the missionaries on the field in 1923, Miss Ward was the recipient of a large, beautiful desk. Of this she wrote:

It was surely one of the biggest joys of my life. To me it indicates the sweet fellowship and fond bond of union that exists between our band of loyal, devoted missionaries.

From Mr. Thuline after furlough:

More Hindus and Mohammedans are dropping into our services than used to come. This is an encouraging sign.

In speaking of one of our India schools, Mr. Puffer writes:

I stood at the door last Sunday morning and watched the

look on the faces of the children as they prayed. I have never at home seen such devotion on the faces of any children while at prayer. How the enemy works to destroy the seed, but in every way we are farther ahead this year than a year ago now. The Taylor Memorial School is a fine school, with good traditions. The agricultural work is going well. Much of the sowing of the cotton was done by the boys. They also are interested in learning about animals. We have purchased a fine line of fowls and milk goats. The weaving has served its main purpose of furnishing our boys with bedding and the chance to make useful things to sell.

From Miss Southworth:

After twenty-seven years in Yeotmal I turned my face toward Wun. The medical work at once took on large proportions. The Christian community of about forty has not been forgotten. During the year I made 124 calls in Christian homes. The spiritual status of the Christians largely regulates the fruit gathered among the heathen.

From Mrs. Davis:

Our second camp-meeting was held in a forest, with a stream of water running through it. All who know how wonderful Ethelbai is with children know they had fine care and instruction. And the parents were enabled to enjoy their own services. At the close of each service the people went off to the jungle to pray; the men on one side of the river and the women on the other. The last Sunday closed with a baptismal service. Three people, all converts from heathenism, were baptized. They were relatives of former converts. This may be our most fruitful way of promulgating our work.

Miss Phelps returning from furlough said:

New bridges have done away with delays for mail because of flooded roads. The new ceiling in the bungalow makes it cooler and safer. The attic is not yet rat-proof. At times it seems as though they were having a national

OUR MISSIONARIES IN INDIA, 1931

ELIZABETH MORELAND

IDA M. MENTOR

ETHEL E. WARD

ADELLA P. CARPENTER

HELEN L. ROOT

convention. The girls in the school have been learning
new kinds of work. They are doing all their own sewing.
One, in particular, has excellent qualities for a nurse.
Eight are teaching Sunday-school classes and are making
good. The greatest change is in the girls themselves.
Christ in the heart transforms the faces of these people.

In December, Miss Phelps again wrote:

For the first time I had the privilege of attending the
National Conference of Trained Nurses. Thirty-five were
present. One of the nice things about being a nurse in
India is realized when traveling. We are granted conces-
sions on nearly all railroads. I am quite happy about moving to Yeotmal to help in the clinics connected with our
school centers. I shall enjoy it more than trying to play
the part of doctor.

In the spring of 1931, Mr. Davis said:

During the last four years the accomplishments of the
Free Methodist Mission in India have in many ways ex-
ceeded those in any preceding quadrennium. The growth
has been healthy and steady. During this time the Lord
has given us three times as many non-Christians as in any
previous four years. Attendance at our school is increasing.
Preachers and Bible women are developing into useful
workers. Many of the laymen are becoming wise counsel-
lors and stanch supporters of the work.

In October, 1931, an Industrial Cooperative Society was
formed in Yeotmal. The shares are ten rupees each, and
one share must be purchased in order to become a member.
The members are mostly Christians of our district. Where
the masses have been suffering for centuries from the deceit
and graft of heartless money-lenders, a well-ordered cooperative movement is a great economic benefit.

In January, 1932, Miss Phelps wrote:

We made "eyes" a special study in our Yeotmal Primary
Schools. I tested the vision of all the children. We also
have made surveys of some villages, as to the number of

blind. We tell them of a land where there is no blindness. "Is it far?" "Does it cost much to go there?"—Questions eagerly asked.

In 1933, Miss Alcorn wrote of changes in Darwha:

Now several trains pass here daily. Motor busses pass our bungalow and stop at our gate, but we still depend upon the faithful oxen for our work among the villages. The fathers and mothers of families here now were children in our orphanages a few years ago. We have a nice crowd of young people, as all are home now for vacation. In a few years this place should become a strong, Christian center.

Late in the year, Mr. Root said:

Our plan this year is to hold evangelistic campaigns in a number of villages. By erecting our large tent in Umbri we have been able to have a series of meetings in spite of the rainy weather. The one young man who was recently saved and baptized is the first convert from Umbri village after twenty-five years of labor here. May this be a year of harvest.

In the spring of 1934, Mr. Puffer said to the Missionary Secretary:

I am now organizing an Educational Cooperative Society. This will help those who need it in financing the education of their children. We feel there is no greater work anywhere than we have right here in Yeotmal in our schools, industries, and financial schemes.

Ernest F. Ward, the veteran missionary to India, returned to America in 1927, having served two score years and more in behalf of India. Silvery white hair, bent shoulders and unsteady hands indicate a life of arduous toil. His intense love for young people makes him a real friend to the students of Los Angeles Pacific College. This aged warrior is an inspiration, as with tracts in hand he treads the streets of Hermon. His courage and faith are a challenge to all who would know the joy of walking with God.

Since 1931 the eldest daughter, Miss Ethel, who has proved herself a worthy example of a second-generation missionary, has cared for the father in their own home.

Our mission in India has taken a leading part in the development of methods of religious education which leads to real Christian experience. Mrs. Puffer has had marked success in this endeavor, not only in Yeotmal but also in the large American Board Mission where Mr. and Mrs. Puffer were called for special service for two years.

Miss Phelps, to relieve the Board, accepted for a time a call to assist in a school for the children of missionaries and other foreign residents in India.

Miss Moreland accepted a position of large influence throughout the whole Marathi area, working for the India Sunday School Union. She retains her relation to our Board and serves our field as well as others.

All agree that India is a difficult field to till. The efforts put forth by the brave men and women have yielded a harvest.

Statistics for 1934 show: Missionaries, 10; stations with resident missionaries, 2; outstations, 4; organized churches, 5; members in full connection, 101; members on probation, 47; Sunday-schools, 22; officers and members, 939; native contributions, $782.00; value of property, $78,800.00.

CHAPTER V

JAPAN

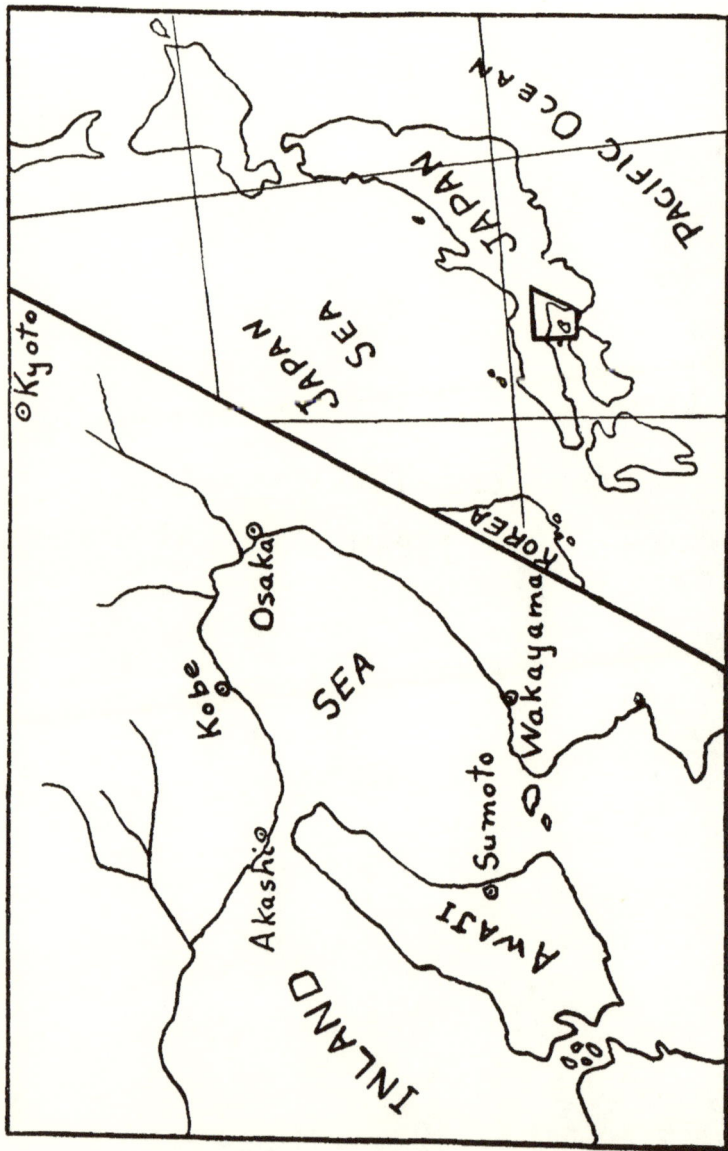

MAP OF OUR JAPAN MISSION FIELD

CHAPTER V

JAPAN

HOW JAPAN OPENED HER DOOR

It was on the blessed Sabbath, on that holy, happy day,
That a fleet of seven warships anchor cast in Yeddo Bay;
'Twas a day that marked a crisis in the history of man,
For America was knocking at the closed door of Japan:
And the brave Commander Perry at the portal was to claim
Right of entrance and protection, in his country's honored
    name.
On the capstan of his vessel were the stars and stripes out-
    spread—
Flag of brotherhood and union! flag for which the brave
    have bled!
And upon that well-loved banner was the open Bible laid—
Book that tells of one great Father, who has all earth's races
    made!
Then the voice of praise and worship rose upon the Lord's
    day calm;
Reverently the good commander read the joyous hundredth
    Psalm;
And the brave notes of "Old Hundred" floated out across
    the Bay,
Drifting, dying in the distance, on the waters far away.
Not a hostile gun was fired, from the fleet or from the shore;
But to Christian hymns of praise open swung the long-closed
    door.   —*Selected.*

IT WAS in 1853 that Japan opened her doors that had been closed for more than 200 years. Missionaries were among the first to enter. It was more than two score years later that the project of Free Methodist missions was launched in the Sunrise Kingdom.

1895-1905

	Began Service	Left	Died
Masazi Kakihara (Paul)	Dec., 1895	1898	
Teikich Kawabe	1896		
Wesley F. Matthewson	Jan., 1903	1908	
Minnie W. Matthewson	" "	"	
August Youngren	" "		1920
Anna Millican Youngren	" "	"	

It was in the second decade of our story that the initial step was taken in Japan. Unlike our other fields the work was begun by its own people.

Masazi Kakihara, while clinging to a ship-wrecked vessel bound for America, experienced the blessing of a clean heart. Providentially he was led to the home of Rev. F. D. Christie in Arizona. There he received the name of Paul as his American name. He was influenced to attend Greenville College, where he remained for two years. He was a young man of more than ordinary intelligence, and his testimony of God's power to save had a marked effect upon congregations. He was eager to start a Free Methodist Mission in his native land.

In 1895 he was accepted by our Board, and President Hogue of Greenville College and Rev. F. H. Ashcraft were appointed to raise money for his passage to Japan. He began work on the west coast of the little Island of Awaji. It was here he met Rev. T. Kawabe. This man had come to America in 1884 to make his fortune. He was then twenty-one years old. He testifies that his religion was only in his head until Thanksgiving day, 1887, when Christ Jesus spoke peace to his troubled heart. The

Lord led him from his successful business career into the gospel ministry. He preached among the Japanese in several places on the Coast and many were led to Christ. His experience leading to heart purity was marvelous. His preaching from that day was productive of wonderful results. After a time a great burden come upon him for the perishing souls of Japan. From an unthought of source funds came to him for his return passage. That was in March, 1893. In the intervening time before meeting Brother Paul, Mr. Kawabe with two helpers had visited every family on the Island of Awaji, praying with the people, and leaving tracts and scripture portions.

These two men were interested in a great, common cause. That same year Mr. and Mrs. Kawabe were accepted by our Board as missionaries on trial.

In 1898 Paul again came to America to attend the General Conference in Chicago. After returning to Japan he soon engaged in a business venture, hoping to increase the funds for missions. Not only was he disappointed in this but became heavily involved in debt. Becoming discouraged he soon severed his connection with our mission. However, Brother Paul made a large contribution to the work by finding Teikich Kawabe, for this man has been the backbone of Free Methodism in Japan. Much of the success attained has been due to the wise counsel and faithful labors of this Spirit-filled man and his wife.

The Board now fearing the results of the undertaking, withheld support for a time, and advised the workers to join another mission. This they declined to do, but kept praying for missionaries to be sent. Prayer and sacrifice saved the day. Some sold their books and other possessions to maintain the work.

In the autumn of 1899 the Missionary Secretary, Rev. B. Winget, visited the field and brought a favorable report to the Board. A call was made for missionaries, to which many responses came.

Mr. Kawabe having a desire to open work in Osaka, the commercial center of the empire, moved there in 1903 and rented a small building near the International Exposition then in progress. It was here that the nucleus of the present Osaka church was formed.

In September of the same year, Mr. and Mrs. Youngren with native help opened the work at Sumoto, the principal town of the Island of Awaji. The following month Mr. and Mrs. Matthewson moved to Osaka and entered whole-heartedly into the task assigned them.

It was also in 1903 that daily Bible study under the leadership of Mr. Kawabe was begun. From this developed the Osaka Bible Training School.

1905-1915

	Began Service		Left	Died
Sherman E. Cooper	February, 1906		1915	
Rose Loomis Cooper	"	"	"	
Minnie K. Hessler	October, 1907		1923	
W. L. Meikle	"	1908	1916	
Grace Livingston Meikle	"	"	"	
Matthias Klein	March	"	1912	
Harriet Cone Klein	"	"	"	

	Began Service	Left	Died
Ruth Mylander	November, 1909		
Roy Millican	" 1911	1928	
Eva Bryan Millican	" "	"	

In 1907, two mission dwelling-houses—one at Osaka and one at Sumoto—were dedicated. Work on the Banshu District was opened in 1907. This is the best farming district in the country. The main line of the railway with branch lines makes travel convenient to the principal villages.

Mr. and Mrs. Klein joined our forces on the field, having been connected previously with another organization. The funds for Miss Mylander's outgoing and stay for many years on the field were donated by her father. In 1911 Bishop Sellew visited the field. His counsel was an inspiration to the workers.

1915-1925

	Began Service	Left	Died
Oliver Haslam	April 1918	1922	
Rachel Becraft Haslam	" "	"	
Lillian O. Pickens	September "		
H. H. Wagner	July 1919		
Gladys Wagner	" "		
Gertrude Aylard	August 1920	1926	

Bible classes in English and cooking classes for the women combined with religious instruction proved a wedge for the entrance of the gospel.

In a letter from Mrs. Cooper, she said:

When a missionary goes into a new community, a crowd of children soon gather around him and his workers. They enjoy music and readily memorize the songs. When a meeting is announced in some house, they crowd ahead of grown folk and generally fill up all the space. So the service for the children is held first.

The work in match factories and cotton spinning factories is largely carried on by child labor. Special meetings are held for these children. Almost exhausted from overwork, some of their little heads can not keep from nodding. Eagerly they join in the singing and give attention to the message.

Mr. Cooper filled a large place in the development of the work in this decade. Of the work at Akashi he wrote: "A continuous revival spirit prevails."

Tetsuji Tsuchiyama was born in a Buddhist home. His parents were bitterly opposed to Christianity. Soon after the glorious victory at Port Arthur in 1905, he with many others was fired with an ambition to perform great tasks. He decided to come to America and become a rich man. Sickness, disappointment and loneliness awaited him in California.

One day a great longing came into his heart that was never satisfied until the night of his conversion in a little Japanese mission in April, 1908. Three years later he experienced a clean heart. Clearly he heard the voice of God calling him to preach the gospel. Like the disciples of old, he heard and followed.

Overcoming every difficulty that beset his path, Mr. Tsuchiyama finished his high school course, received his college degree, and entered Drew Theological Seminary.

By a peculiar providence this choice young man became acquainted with our people and joined the Free Methodist Church in 1917.

In April, 1918, Tetsuji Tsuchiyama was graduated from Drew Theological Seminary. Of his sermon before the seniors a classmate said, "You are the first one who shook the foundation of our chapel." Though receiving many handsome opportunities, he answered God's call to return to Japan just in time for the opening of school, and was welcomed by the missionaries, as they had anticipated the arrival of this promising worker.

On October 28, 1918, he was married to one of the Osaka Bible women, who had been Miss Mylander's assistant. The ceremony was performed in the Osaka church by Rev. T. Kawabe. Congratulations and a wedding sermon followed. In another building the invited guests later partook of a feast.

In 1920, Mr. Youngren wrote as follows:

On the Banshu District we have one main station, Akashi, and four outstations, all conveniently located. We hope to make Akashi a strong center. I visit the Island of Awaji and hold the quarterly meetings. It is difficult for Miss Hessler, a single woman, to have charge of that district, but she has done well and has worked faithfully.

That same year, Rev. W. B. Olmstead and wife, and Rev. L. Glenn Lewis and wife, sailed to Japan as delegates to the World's Sunday School Convention in Tokyo. They visited each mission station.

In 1921, Mrs. Millican in writing of the Sunday-schools said:

The one in Osaka had the distinction of being represented in Tokyo as one of the two model Sunday-schools of Japan. Brother Tsuchiyama is the superintendent. There are eight branch schools. It was an inspiring sight to see several hundred little brown faces and hear their sweet voices sing of the wonderful Christ-child at the Christmas exercises.

As they entered the church, each child was given a piece of newspaper in which he wrapped his wooden shoes or clogs and carried them to his seat. This was to prevent confusion and to avoid the possibility of any shoes being lost. One number of the program was a song in English by the English Bible classes taught by the Misses Aylard, Pickens and Mylander. Thirty of the teachers and officers sang, "Holy Night," carrying the four parts very well. Those who had been in attendance regularly for a year were given prizes—there were seventy of these, and five who had not missed for five years. The next evening the grown people celebrated. Wonderful testimonies were given. One sister received a reward for not having been absent once in ten years.

In January, 1921, Miss Pickens wrote:

It is a privilege to be here at a time when the need is so great. We work among such a refined class of people that it is hard to believe the terrible things we read in the newspapers about the Japanese.

Our church is the only one which is doing anything to save the hundreds who visit the nearby picture shows every night. Over 30,000 hear the gospel in our chapel every year. With many of them it is the first time.

In March, 1921, Rev. and Mrs. T. Kawabe sailed for America, planning to spend five months on the Pacific coast and then travel east.

Mr. Wagner, in writing of the Sumoto meeting held in the new tent sent from America, said:

Between our house and the shore of the Pacific there is a park filled with beautiful trees. Among these trees we erected the tent. The meeting was in July, one of the hottest months of the year, hence hundreds of people came here to the beach. This gave us a fine opportunity. The people would stand attentively for a long time. How young and old listened to the Bible stories in the children's meetings! It was a glorious ten-days' revival.

The Osaka Training School had never been properly housed and equipped. The location was unfavorable and the buildings too small. In 1920 the Board authorized the sale of the old property and the purchase of a new site. This was done, but money for the buildings was not available.

The Japanese Provisional Conference was organized in September, 1923, by W. B. Olmstead. Rev. T. Kawabe was elected district elder for the three districts.

On September 1, 1923, Japan suffered a terrible disaster by earthquake. Yokohama and Tokyo were nearly destroyed. Miss Aylard wrote:

How thankful we are that none of our work was damaged and all the missionaries are safe, and yet we can not but feel for those missions that lost so much.

In 1923 Miss Hessler retired, having spent sixteen successful years on the field. Later she became the wife of Walter A. Morse.

At the annual session of the Genesee Conference in 1923, Mitsu Kawabe was ordained to deacon's and elder's orders by Bishop Clark. Mr. Kawabe had received his A.B. degree at Greenville College in 1920, finished his course at Drew Theological Seminary in 1923, and was given a scholarship at Edinburgh University, Scotland, for a year of study.

In December, 1923, the first Free Methodist Church of Osaka burned. The pastor lost a choice selection of books. The origin of the fire was unknown.

In 1924 a lot was purchased in Kobe upon which to build a modern home for the superintendent.

1925-1935

	Began Service	Left	Died
Frank Warren	August, 1925		
Lucile Secord Warren	" "		

At the urgent request of the missionaries, the Missionary Secretary again visited the field and held the annual conference in 1925. He planned for the new school building and the advancement of the work in general.

After returning from Japan in 1926, Mrs. Sellew said:

One of the things that impressed me was the way the women are taking their place in the church. I never spoke to a more interested group than the one gathered to hear me in the First Church, Osaka. I was much pleased with the location chosen for the Bible Training School and Missionary Home, but was depressed when I heard there was thought of selling the front in order to get money with which to build.

It was through the prayers and efforts of Mrs. Sellew that the situation was saved.

Mrs. Millican concerning the Training School said:

Two-thirds of the preachers and their wives, also single evangelists and Bible women in the Japan Conference, have received their training in this school. The success of our work is due as much, if not more, to the work of this school than to any other factor.

In a letter from Mr. Warren we quote:

Our trip across the ocean was marred by some mission-

REV. AND MRS. TEIKICH KAWABE

REV. AND MRS. T. TSUCHIYAMA AND FAMILY

aries who insisted that of all people the Japanese are the worst. My heart is deeply stirred when I read the unfounded criticisms of this people. We find them to be most kind, courteous and thoughtful. I am led to think many times that Jesus was in a very real sense an Oriental. The great need of Japan is Christianity, and we as a church are putting first things first. Other missions speak highly of our evangelism and envy us our spiritual leaders.

Again from Mr. Warren:

The newness has worn off and we are gradually beginning to feel ourselves at home. We are working to the utmost of our capacity on the language. I wonder if the people at home realize just what a stupendous task it is to get a foreign language as difficult as the Japanese. We are conscious that only as God helps us can we master it.

In November, 1926, Mr. Millican wrote:

Today I signed the contract for two buildings, the Administration and Boys' Dormitory. The ground is to be staked off next Tuesday. It is expected that the buildings will be ready for Commencement in March.

Much credit is due Mr. Millican for his skill in promoting the building projects during his term of service.

Bishop William Pearce held the Japan Conference in the spring of 1927. His labors were appreciated by all who were touched by his ministry.

Mr. Tsuchiyama was chosen delegate from Japan to the General Conference in Rochester, New York, in June, 1927. The following year was spent at Princeton Seminary. On the return journey he visited Egypt and Palestine. His addresses and spirit of humility will long be remembered.

In July, 1928, Mr. Warren, having moved to Sumoto into the house vacated by the Wagner family on furlough, wrote:

We are comfortably situated in the loveliest spot in Japan. The last thing we hear at night is the break of the waves on our lovely beach just a few hundred feet from the house. We are praying that our service may be in keeping with the beauty of our surroundings.

In Mr. Wagner's Sunday-school at Ikuro for three successive years twenty of the children did not miss a meeting. This Sunday-school was started by a converted policeman. It is now a self-supporting church.

In the spring of 1929, the Missionary Secretary again visited Japan, and presided at the annual conference. He wrote:

There was a forward movement all along the line among the missionaries and the preachers. Four years ago the first church building was in ruins, but out of the ashes has arisen one of the finest and most serviceable buildings in our denomination. This society has been entirely self-supporting since 1920, and the new building was erected by the Japanese people. Fifty adults are to be baptized on Easter Sunday.

The kindergarten project was launched in 1929, and the first class was graduated in March, 1930. A small three-room house was erected on the campus in Osaka for this purpose. The Board paid half of the cost and the Japanese Christians the remainder. Mrs. Tsuchiyama, the mother of six children, was the head of this school. She and her assistant, Mrs. Hitomi, held kindergarten certificates recognized by the government. At great sacrifice these noble women gave their time to this work. Mrs. Tsuchiyama received no salary. Thus the school was self-supporting, the tuitions having more than paid all the running expenses. Many of the mothers attend the cooking class and hear the gospel. Several have been converted. Now the building has been enlarged and is adequate to meet the needs.

The little town of Fukura on the west coast of the Island of Awaji was the birthplace of Free Methodism in Japan. In 1929 Brother Endo, the pastor-elder, undertook to do the seemingly impossible—the building of a suitable church—and succeeded.

Although the rain was pouring in torrents the evening of the dedication, every seat was filled and some were standing. Mr. Kawabe preached the sermon and told of his early experiences. The mayor, who was present, said the building was a splendid asset to the town. There are few towns of its size that can boast of such a well-equipped, pleasant building.

In March, 1931, Mr. Warren wrote:

For two years we have tried to have a mass meeting of Awaji Christians. It seemed an impossibility. How could it be financed? The meeting just closed and it surpassed all expectation. Never was there such a melting time on the part of the Christians. People gave as they have not given before. If you think hard times have come to America, remember the majority of these people have all their lives known nothing else. The last service was unique in its conclusion. Instead of quietly and politely bowing to one another and leaving, they lingered to shake hands in good Free Methodist style. We had seen nothing like it before in our five and one-half years in Japan.

In March, 1931, Miss Mylander returned to

America on account of the illness of her sister. Now the way seems clear for her return.

In the spring of 1931, Bishop and Mrs. Griffith visited Japan and were given a hearty welcome. Bishop Griffith presided over the conference and Mrs. Griffith was an inspiration to the women.

In December, 1931, Mr. Kawabe preached his last sermon as active pastor of the First Church of Osaka. Twenty-seven years is a long time for a Free Methodist pastor to serve one church. The last year was one of great trial, but his conference report showed forty-two members in full connection and 275 probationers. The most fruitful years of his long life were given to this church. He has always been an evangelist and his people have been willing to have him away often. Eternity alone will reveal the influence of this one church. Brother Kawabe is known and respected throughout the Empire. Many times he has preached over the radio, and has addressed great mass meetings. His sermons are full of apt illustrations. He wishes to spend his remaining years in special meetings, writing and prayer.

The great work of Mrs. Kawabe has been with the women. She knows how to lead them step by step to belief in Jesus Christ.

When the Japanese preachers heard of our financial depression in 1932, they called a meeting and spent two full days together. They decided to relinquish the salaries they were receiving from America and rely fully on their own people for their support. Mr. Warren said, "Such willingness to sacrifice has never been seen before in our work."

In February, 1934, Mrs. Tsuchiyama closed her eyes to earthly scenes and labors. In tributes from missionaries we glean:

Mrs. Tsuchiyama, endowed with more than ordinary native ability, was one of a thousand. The church-members constantly sought her advice in temporal as well as spiritual matters. She was the foreigners' friend. Many times her tactful explanation to our Japanese acquaintances relieved a strained situation.

The Osaka Seminary, of which Mr. Tsuchiyama is president, has grown rapidly, assuming a place of leadership among the holiness schools in Japan. At the Foreign Missions Conference in New York City a year ago, favorable mention was made of this school.

In 1932, Mr. Tsuchiyama was elected traveling elder. A part of each week he spends on the field. He is a mighty preacher of the gospel. He has no doubts to weaken his efforts. His teaching shows long and careful preparation. Despite the honors thrust upon him, he is humble and a stanch defender of Free Methodism.

It is a cause for rejoicing that the church of Japan, purged of the leaven of modernism, can be safely trusted with the reins of leadership. Today the majority of organized churches are meeting all or more than half of their local expenses. There are three times as many Japanese in the Bible School preparing for Christian work today as a decade ago. There has been a steady, healthy growth.

It is nothing less than miraculous the way the Japanese missionaries are enabled to carry the financial burden of their work without help from the homeland. Their numbers are increasing and they are growing in grace and in knowledge of the Lord Jesus Christ.

1934 statistics show: Missionaries, 3; stations with resident missionaries, 22; outstations, 4; organized churches, 25; members in full connection, 1,085; members on probation, 819; Sunday-schools, 37; officers and members, 2,313; native contributions, $13,618.50; value of property, $176,375.00.

CHAPTER VI

CHINA

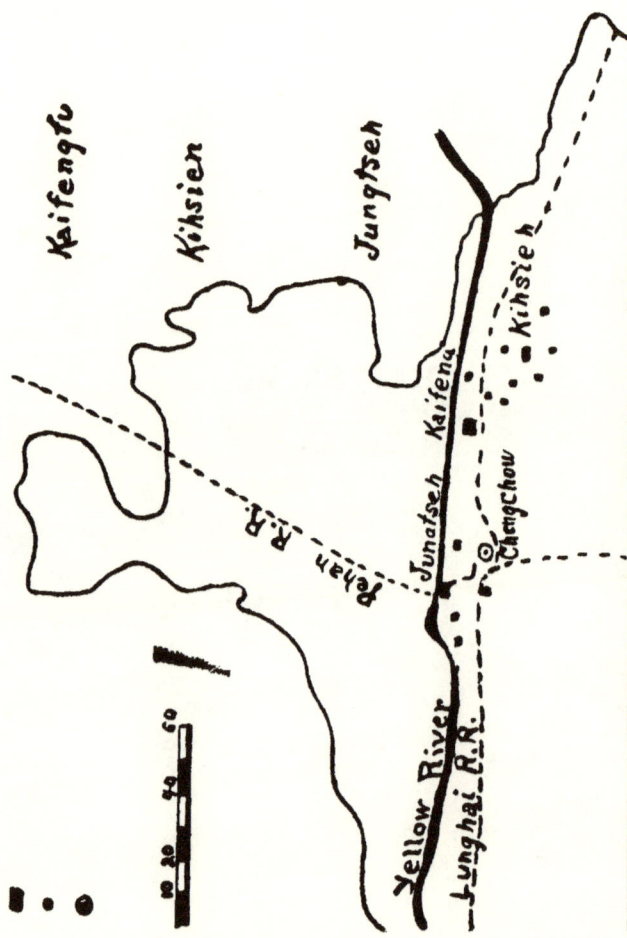

Kaifengfu

Kihsien

Jungtseh

Yellow River

Lunghai R.R.

Pehan R.R.

Jungtseh

Kaifeng

Chengchow

Kihsieh

10 20 30 40 50 60

MAP OF OUR MISSION STATIONS IN CHINA

CHAPTER VI

CHINA

1895-1905

	Began Service	Left	Died
C. Floyd Appleton	November, 1904	1920	1932
G. H. Scofield	" 1904	1919	

TO the thoughtful, unusual young woman—Clara Leffingwell—came the conviction in 1895 that God would have her serve in behalf of China. Our Board not seeing its way clear to establish a mission in that country at that time, she went out under the China Inland Mission in January, 1896. She was sent into the interior, and endured many testing and thrilling experiences connected with the Boxer trouble. At the close of a term of seven years she returned to America in May, 1903.

In 1899 Rev. B. Winget, the Missionary Secretary, corresponded with Miss Leffingwell as to the advisability and cost of starting a mission in China. That same year while visiting the Japan field, Mr. Winget went to Shanghai to confer with the leaders of the China Inland Mission as to the possibilities of a denominational mission.

In June, 1903, at the General Conference in Greenville, Illinois, the Board ordered the secretary to open a mission as soon as possible. Miss Leffingwell being in this country was authorized to travel throughout the church in the interests of the project. The two taxing years spent in this service were possibly the most fruitful years of her life. Her stirring appeals encouraged large gifts. These were augmented by a substantial sum from the contingent fund of the Woman's Missionary Society, also by a gift of $5,000 from Mr. N. B. Peterson of Seattle.

The first missionaries to reach the field landed at Shanghai on the last day of 1904. They proceeded up the Yangste river beyond Hankow, then farther on into the mountains of Swechuan Province to study the language among the native people.

1905-1915

	Began Service		Left	Died
Clara Leffingwell	April	1905		1905
Edith D. Graves	"	"	1907	
Florence R. Myers	"	"	1919	
N. S. Honn	September	"	1912	
Alice Griffith Honn	"	"	"	
Laura E. Millican	February,	1906	1920	
Lily M. Peterson	"	"		1908
Edith Frances Jones	October,	1907		
Lucy A. Tittemore	"	"	1920	
Frank R. Millican	"	"	1916	
Aimee Boddy Millican	"	"	"	
F. J. Fletcher and wife		1908		
George Schlosser		"		
Mary Ogren (Schlosser)	Sept.,	1909		
Mattie J. Peterson	"	"		
Maud W. Edwards	"	1911		1933
Dr. A. L. Grinnell	August,	1912		1923

Maud Grinnell   August, 1912   1927
Letitia Chandler   January, 1913
Grace M. Stewart, R.N.   May   1914   1916

Miss Leffingwell with her two helpers arrived in Shanghai in May, 1905. After a journey of 500 miles they reached Chengchow, twelve miles south of the Yellow River, in the Province of Honan, where it had been decided to locate. Having rented a small compound just inside the north gate of the city, Miss Leffingwell superintended the necessary repairs, and preached to the people as she was able.

On July 4 she was taken violently ill. Doctors and a nurse were summoned. The strain of the work, lack of proper food and the intense heat made her an easy victim. On July 16, she passed away and was buried outside the city gate among the Chinese graves. Later a cemetery was provided by gifts from Miss Leffingwell's sister and friends. To those who remained she left "a precious memory and a great task."

Before the young men from the distant province could arrive, the two young women had gone to the hill station for language study. Mr. Appleton was made superintendent of the mission.

It was in October of the same year that Mr. and Mrs. Honn from California, with four of their children, arrived. They had labored among the Chinese on the Pacific Coast and were somewhat familiar with the language.

The following winter a compound nearer the center of the city was purchased and repaired and the Honn family took charge of the station.

Bishop and Mrs. W. A. Sellew visited the field early in 1906 and assisted in solving some of the difficult problems. Property was purchased at Jungtseh Hsien, fifteen miles northwest of Chengchow. The first Free Methodist class was organized there with Mr. Scofield in charge. He and Miss Myers were united in marriage that year, and the following year occurred the marriage of Mr. Appleton and Miss Millican. They opened the work in Kaifeng, which became the headquarters of the mission field. It was here the Empress Dowager fled, when the allied troops captured Peking in 1900. At one time Kaifeng was the capital of all China.

In the spring of 1907 some of our missionaries attended the celebration of A Century of Protestant Missions in China at Shanghai. This was an inspiring event to our pioneers.

This was also a year of great floods and famine. The *Christian Herald* undertook extensive relief work, and our mission agreed to care for sixty orphans. These were in charge of Rev. and Mrs. F. J. Fletcher, who came under our Board while on the field. Mr. Schlosser who had recently transferred from our African mission was appointed to assist them. The project was carried on at Tsingkiang.

The missionaries suffered much from illness during this period. In 1907, Miss Graves finding the work too taxing for her strength, reluctantly returned to the homeland. Miss Lily Peterson was obliged to return in 1908 and soon fell asleep to wake in a fairer clime. Her influence in China still lives. Mr. Appleton, having suffered a severe attack of typhoid fever, returned for furlough in 1910.

Mr. Scofield also contracted the disease and was obliged to go home for a time.

In 1909 the China Inland Mission turned over to our Board a small outstation at Kihsien, thirty miles southeast of Kaifeng. Mr. and Mrs. Millican labored there for some time.

Mr. Schlosser and Miss Ogren were united in marriage in 1911. They remained in charge of the orphanage until it was discontinued in 1914.

Early in this year, Bishop and Mrs. Sellew again visited China, partly at their own expense. Many lasting benefits resulted from this trip.

In 1911 China was in the throes of a revolution. Most missionaries were ordered from their stations. Some of other denominations were massacred. War raged in the Yangtse valley. Hankow was burned. In March, 1912, the Empress Dowager and the Emperor abdicated and China was declared a republic. Restrictions were soon removed, but conditions remained unsettled for a long time. In a few months missionaries were permitted to return to their stations.

The arrival of a medical missionary and family brought cheer to the band of workers. For a time Dr. Grinnell assisted in the China Inland Mission Hospital.

Early in 1913, the Missionary Secretary, Mr. Winget, and wife again visited the field and rendered valuable service.

In a letter from Miss Tittemore she said:

We have just had a week of special meetings and classes for believers and inquirers who live in the country. About thirty men and nearly as many women came. Mrs. Schlosser had a class on the Discipline for women. Christmas week was the coldest weather I have ever seen in China. As there was no rain the latter part of the summer, the fields are bare instead of green with wheat as usual.

1915-1925

	Began Service		Left	Died
I. S. W. Ryding	October,	1916		
Edwin P. Ashcraft	November	"		
Harriet Ashcraft	"	"		
Bernice M. Wood	"	"		
Jacob Schaffer	December,	1917		
Kate Leininger, R. N.	"	"		
G. L. McClish	August	1918	1923	
Sadie McClish	"	"	"	
Thomas Beare	"	"		1919
Minnie Honn Beare	"	"	1920	
Florence Murray	October	1919		
Geneva Sayre	September,	1921		
Grace Somerville, R. N.	"	"		
Pearl Denbo Schaffer	June	1922		
H. E. Leise	January	1923	1927	
Pearl Mercer Leise	"	"	"	
E. Locke Silva	August	"		
Carrie Coffee Silva	"	"		

In 1916 it was decided to sell the compound at Chengchow and concentrate the few workers at other stations.

Miss Stewart, a trained nurse, made exceptional progress in the language, and assisted in the women's work at Kihsien. At the end of two years she succumbed to typhoid fever.

In the winter of 1916-1917, the Missionary Secretary, Mr. MacGeary, and wife visited the field and stayed some time at each station.

In the autumn of 1917, two and one-half acres of land outside the south gate of Kihsien were purchased for hospital use. The compound walls and gate house were built.

In September, 1918, the first conference of all the Christian workers was held at Kaifeng in the new church. Delegates from places having Sunday services and at least five members were present. Problems were presented and discussed.

In the autumn of 1918, Dr. Grinnell reported that as a result of a terrible storm, the compound wall around the south end of the new hospital building on which he had spent so much labor was nearly all down. The mud wall, not yet dry, could not stand the strain.

In February, 1919, Mr. Ashcraft wrote:

There has been very little wind and dust this winter. On Christmas Eve we had a beautiful snow about five inches deep. We were reminded of Whittier's "Snow Bound."

Bernice Wood to her mother:

Isn't this world-wide epidemic—influenza—a strange thing? I have not lost a day from work and hope to keep my record good. Sometimes we choose to walk on the walls. Off to the west we see mountains. They form a pleasing background for the near-by wheat fields and plains. This has been an excellent year for crops.

I am trying to follow out last Sunday's Golden Text and be "fruitful in that which is least." I am planning for an afternoon "at home" when the women will feel free to come in. Well, "my Father is rich" and I have need of nothing.

In the spring of 1919 from a letter from Miss Leininger we quote:

We have just closed a ten-days' station class for women at Kihsien. About fifty were present. Their lives have been so narrow and cramped. It is a marvel to watch the spiritual growth of these eager learners. A few came as far as twenty miles away. They brought food, fuel, babies and bedding. Some were brought in on wheelbarrows by their husbands.

Pneumonia was the cause of Mr. Beare's sudden death in the fall of 1919. His going was mourned by Christians and non-Christians. Sixteen men carried the coffin to Chengchow, fifteen miles away, to our own cemetery. Three Chinese friends accompanied the procession on foot, while others went by train. The body of the beloved missionary was laid to rest beside the other two graves.

The following spring a son was born to Mrs. Beare—Thomas James Beare, Jr.

In 1920, a Bible Training School for men was opened at Kaifeng. The funds for the building were given by Dr. Blackstone of Los Angeles.

In 1920 there was unusual and severe illness among the missionaries. Many suffered from influenza, some being critically ill. Mrs. Grinnell was low with diptheria. Miss Wood was near death with virulent smallpox. In answer to prayer these lives were spared.

When the Missionary Secretary, W. B. Olmstead, and his wife arrived in China that same year they found the station platform crowded with a seething mass of humanity. An unprecedented famine prevailed. The missionaries were absorbed in the dis-

REV. H. H. WAGNER AND FAMILY

REV. F. F. WARREN AND FAMILY

RUTH MYLANDER, GERTRUDE AYLARD, LILIAN O. PICKENS

CLARA LEFFINGWELL

MAUD EDWARDS

GRINNELL MEMORIAL HOSPITAL.

REV. JAMES H. TAYLOR

REV. E. P. ASHCRAFT

tribution of grain and other necessities. Thousands of lives were touched by the gospel in this ministry of relief.

In 1921, Muh Chen Fan, the oldest worker in point of service and of age, died a triumphant death. He was beloved by the missionaries, by the Chinese Christians and by the unbelievers. He was won from Mohammedanism.

In April, 1921, Miss Edwards wrote:

I'm so glad I'm not on furlough, for surely we never had such an opportunity to reach people as now. This famine has brought many, many to a knowledge of Christ. Many homes have destroyed their gods. We are kept busy in the guest hall and in visiting the homes.

Later Mrs. McClish wrote:

My husband is giving all his time to the famine relief work. Hundreds of people are opening their hearts and homes to us. We have been praying for a revival. This is God's answer.

In February, 1922, Miss Sayre wrote:

Last Sunday was the final and big day of the Chinese New Year's celebration. Every one was supposed to go somewhere and not to work. Thus we had many more people at the mission than usual. There must have been at least 1,000 women who heard the gospel that day and many of them for the first time. When we see how anxious they are to learn, we say, "It pays!"

On account of the constant flooded area, it was decided to change the location of the hospital at Kihsien to within the city walls.

When Mr. Appleton returned to America he left his copy of the church Discipline translated into

Chinese. The ritual was to be completed and the whole to be reviewed by Chinese Christians.

Miss Jones gave much time and energy to the completion of this project, and the finished product in 1922 was a great achievement. It prepared the way for a conference organization.

After six months in China, Miss Sayre wrote:

The native Christians here are a credit to the home church. Salvation is real in China, the same as in America. I feel very much at home and in God's will here.

At the annual meeting in 1922, a delegation of over twenty walked fifty miles to be present. One seventy-nine years old not only walked but wheeled a barrow. Famine conditions continued. People were dying on the streets and babies were being thrown away.

In May, 1922, Mrs. Schlosser wrote:

The wealthy women and girls of the city are flocking to us for refuge, ours being counted the safest place in Kihsien. The city gates are all shut and banked with dirt. Shut up in a Chinese city with 15,000 Chinese and 400 robber soldiers! Praise God for the peace that triumphs over fear and worry!

Mr. Ashcraft writing of Mr. Schlosser said:

He deserves a medal for the way he managed the situation at Kihsien. His past experience in the army stood him in good stead. Both Chinese and foreigners speak of it as a real piece of diplomacy.

In June, 1922, Mr. Jacob Schaffer and Miss Pearl Denbo of the Nazarene Mission were united in marriage. Mrs. Schaffer joined our forces, not as a stranger but as an esteemed friend.

In September Mrs. Grinnell wrote:

The country is passing through a period of unprecedented lawlessness. There seems to be no large part of the country that wholly escapes, but the Province of Honan, in which our work is located, has been one of the worst sufferers.

In November, 1923, the China field suffered a great loss in the death of Dr. Grinnell. He died on his forty-third birthday. With deep concern he relinquished his cherished earthly work. He was buried in the cemetery at Chengchow so sacred to the mission. A missionary friend said of him: "The qualities of the Christian gentleman, in all the social, business, domestic and professional relationships of life, were manifested by him in a rare degree." As a medical pioneer he did a great work.

In the autumn of 1923, Rev. and Mrs. W. B. Olmstead visited the missions in China. Their messages and counsel were an inspiration to the missionaries and also to the native Christians. A real knowledge of the field and its possibilities was obtained.

In 1924, Mr. Schlosser writing of the remodeled Kihsien church said:

The money raised by the Chinese would amount to what $100 in gold would per member at home. Also the missionaries came nobly to share in the burden.

1925-1935

	Began Service		Left	Died
Harry Green	August	1925	1927	
Dr. Alta Sager Green	"	"	"	
Bessie C. Reid	"	"		

Grace Murray, R. N. September, 1926   1934
James Hudson Taylor   "   "
Alice Hayes Taylor   "   "
Dr. John Dryer Green   "   1932
Lydia F. Green, R. N.   "   "
Pearl M. Reid, R. N.   "   1934

In January, 1925, Mr. Ryding wrote:

China is still in the throes of widespread Civil War. Several cities in Honan have been sacked by soldiers recently. So far our work has not been hindered.

From Miss Edwards:

It makes me very happy to see how the Christians give of their time. There are forty of sixty members here at Jungtseh this morning putting down a well. It is all hand work in China. They use no machinery. They come up drenched with mud and water. The Chinese are clever people and know how to *do* things. I believe this is the gladdest, happiest time of my life.

In May, 1925, Grandma Jones from Jamestown, New York, mother of Miss Edith Frances Jones, fell asleep in Jesus. She had gone to China with her daughter when returning from furlough. She was loved by the Chinese and always exerted a refining influence. She was buried at Chengchow in that beautiful cemetery with the missionaries. As one said, "Her dust sleeps as peacefully there as it would at Jamestown, New York."

June 10, 1925, at Potomac Avenue church, Buffalo, New York, Mr. Harry J. Green and Dr. Alta Sager were united in marriage. They with Mr. Green's son sailed for China in August, 1925.

Dr. Green wrote after the siege of Tientsin:

We have been helping in the big base hospital located six miles from Peking. Mr. Green and I had prayers each morning as I went out, and am glad to say that so far God has not permitted me to have a single death on the table while dressing wounds. The government students had planned a big anti-Christian demonstration for Christmas day, but it did not occur.

From Miss Edwards:

We have had two lovely snow storms this winter, which were like just so much money falling down from heaven as there was no rain during the fall. I never loved my Chinese women as I love them now.

From Mr. Ryding:

We have a large tent with which we are evangelizing among the countless villages. Many idols have been taken down. It is Chinese New Year season. It is observed by the Christian church as a special week of evangelism. The whole region is terrorized by hordes of soldiers. A Chinese soldier sometimes shows himself a friend.

From Mrs. Silva in March, 1926:

These are strenuous days, and the heat is upon us. Am able to keep up my duties. I teach two classes a week in the girls' day school, oversee the school, teach a Sunday-school class, lead a class-meeting, besides going to the women's meetings. We are contented in Him.

It was in October, 1926, that Mr. Ryding was captured by brigands. Many throughout the denomination heard him speak while on furlough, telling of his terrorizing experiences during those twelve days of agony and suspense. Through the efforts of Mr. Silva and Mr. Schlosser, the authorities at Kaifeng obtained his release. God heard and answered. Later he wrote:

The day after I reached home a thanksgiving service

was held. We are resolved anew to do our best to rescue men and women from sin. There is perpetual Civil War. There are probably many more soldiers in Honan now than in the standing army of the United States. Many at heart are no better than brigands. But these conditions can be changed! May a great volume of public and private intercession ascend from the church.

In March, 1927, the following cablegram was received at headquarters from Mr. Ashcraft:

Considering the present circumstances all have gone to Peking.

In December Mr. Ashcraft wrote:

Soldiers moved out of the house! We have had a busy day getting settled. Really feel at home. I am in the sitting room with a nice fire. Here there has been very little loss from looting, but at Kihsien everything has been taken from each of our mission houses, including the hospital. Even the door locks are missing. To our Christians all this was a very severe test. However, nearly all stood faithful. Only one evangelist betrayed his trust. The missionaries of other Boards sought our Christian men as messengers, saying, "They can be trusted."

Again in February, 1928, from Mr. Ashcraft:

The conditions now in Honan, so far as I see, are not much different than when we left a year ago. Our mission is perhaps suffering less than any other in this section, the Roman Catholic not excepted. God has a way through.

In June, 1928, Miss Wood wrote:

Grasshoppers are the latest excitement in these parts. One village brought in twenty-four pounds of the pests which they had caught and turned over to the Jungtseh official. We had a special season of prayer about this new calamity. Thermometer registers 104 in the shade this afternoon.

From Miss Leininger:

At last all of our buildings at Kihsien have been vacated by soldiers. Much credit is due our faithful gatekeeper for his services during the past year of trouble and unrest. He told us that many nights he scarcely slept at all as he felt so keenly his responsibility.

In January, 1929, little Jeannie Taylor, daughter of Rev. and Mrs. J. H. Taylor, went to be with Jesus. She was a wealth of sunshine to all the missionaries.

Mrs. Schlosser wrote:

The forming of our first annual conference and the meetings, both business and inspirational, are a matter of history. The going of Brother Olmstead from station to station involved many days of arduous travel by rickshaw, through roads deep with sand and dust, and with a bad dust storm every other day or so. Chinese and foreigners alike feel we have taken a great step forward.

In February, 1930, Miss Peterson wrote:

It has been a very trying ordeal. Brother Ashcraft helped out at Jungtseh during the weeks of special stress and strain. He was able to do a great deal of personal work with officers and soldiers and had daily meetings with them. We believe God will bring fruit from this sowing. Our God is a God of deliverances.

In May, 1930, Mrs. Schlosser said of the second annual conference:

It wasn't just a conference—it was a revival—and the presence of the Lord carried the conference right along. Brother Ashcraft in presiding was given physical strength and wisdom. The idea of self-support is beginning to take hold. As one expressed it, "We feel as if things are getting on a solid foundation now!"

In 1930 our original compound in the city of

Chengchow was bought back. The deed had never been changed. It is now named the Leffingwell Compound.

Miss Sayre said:

With all the sentiment attached to this place, I am pleased to live here. The Chinese buildings at the back of the compound have been repaired. The people are most friendly.

From Miss Somerville:

The Bible woman and I have been having classes for two weeks at one of the outstations. In one class there were three women over seventy and one blind woman. They will never be able to learn to read, but we want them to know about the Bible, so the Bible woman started in with Genesis and gave each chapter in story form, giving two lessons a day. They were greatly interested. We also had a class of women in the thirties and a few girls in their teens.

In August, 1930, Mrs. Taylor wrote:

Since April, Honan has been ravished by war. The two best trained armies in China are matched against each other. Kaifeng and Kihsien have had frequent visits from them. It is marvelous how we have been preserved.

In February, 1931, Miss Chandler wrote:

It has been a cold winter with much snow. It is near the end of the old Chinese year. Today the kitchen god is burned, thus sending it up to heaven. A number of families have destroyed their idols. A young man who was addicted to opium-smoking has been saved and delivered from the habit.

That year the conference was presided over by Bishop G. W. Griffith. He was accompanied by Mrs. Griffith, who greatly aided the women and young people in their societies. Bishop Griffith said:

CHINA   121

It is my deliberate conviction that China presents to the church of Christ today one of the most pressing challenges in the history of the Christian church. Temples and shrines are slowly disintegrating. Idols are broken or destitute of worshipers. It is China's hour to receive the gospel. Communism will win the day unless Christ comes to China today.

In May, 1932, occurred the death of Rev. C. Floyd Appleton in Seattle. He spent two terms in China under our Board, serving as superintendent most of the time. His service was marked by sacrifice and faithfulness.

From Miss Florence Murray:

We have recently prepared a Home Study Course for children. This includes in part the memorizing of considerable scripture, the names of the books of the Bible, the learning of twelve hymns, and the reading of a number of books.

In August, 1933, Miss Maud Edwards, after twenty-two years of service, left earthly toil for heaven. Her merry heart, her never-failing patience and kindness, made her a choice companion and a joy to the Chinese women among whom she labored. When on furlough she would say, "I am homesick for China."

In February, 1934, Miss Grace Murray, while home on furlough, died in Highland, Illinois, following an operation for appendicitis. In tributes from the missionaries we glean: "Her life was a sweet fragrance. In unselfish service and as a nurse she excelled. She has a big place in the hearts of the Chinese. The church has lost a great missionary." She directed that $2,000 of her estate should finance her successor to her chosen field.

In 1934, Mr. Taylor wrote:

Last year the China Conference launched a new venture. We decided to carry the gospel into new fields. This project was to be undertaken by the church in China. It was our privilege to visit Fengchin, our first outpost north of the Yellow river. The spiritual atmosphere was most encouraging. Three joined on probation. A storekeeper burned twenty packages of cigarets instead of selling them.

From the report of the 1934 annual conference we glean the following:

Crowds from all directions arrived. Sixty old ladies walked fifteen miles. At the evangelistic services the church was full to overflowing, aisles, windows and doors being packed. Many times all prayed at once. Our Chinese are taking up the load and proving themselves equal to the responsibilities placed upon them. We were made to rejoice over the gains and victories of the past year. Both the W. M. S. and the Y. P. M. S. had their business meetings. Gains have been made in each. All have returned to their same work for another year with new courage and faith.

Mrs. Green, in writing of the hospital, says:

The doctor has sufficient knowledge of the language so that he can converse with the people and is ready to commence the work for which the church commissioned him. This building is to be the dispensary. There will be a waiting-room where the evangelist will tell the story of Christ to the people as they wait their turns. There will be an examining room where the doctor with a Chinese assistant will decide upon the needed treatment. There will be a small laboratory, and another room where minor surgery can be done and drugs dispensed. With surprisingly little cleaning and remodeling they can be ready for use. There are thousands of waiting patients with all manner of chronic and acute diseases. Many are members of our church. The end in view is that many who come for physical healing may find the Lord as a personal Savior. Doctor, hospital, patients—but not sufficient money for equipment, supplies, drugs.

The work of the China mission is mainly evangelistic. After the revolution the government took over the work of education and refused to allow religious instruction in registered schools. Hence our educational work is limited to the Training Schools and the Girls' Orphanage. These are not registered and are free to teach the Bible.

The Kaifeng Bible School for Men is a growing institution. Rev. C. F. Appleton and Rev. E. P. Ashcraft each had a part in laying the foundations. Rev. Jacob H. Schaffer, the unremitting toiler, was the first principal. A class of five was graduated in 1923. While Mr. Schaffer was on furlough, Miss Jones ably guided affairs, but during the evacuation of 1927 the class of that year was widely scattered. Later when the school was reopened, five were graduated in 1930.

Twenty-five students were registered in September, 1934. Life investments in this school are paying high dividends.

The Women's Bible School has grown rapidly during this decade. The regular course in the Bible School covers three years and includes intensive courses in Old and New Testament, Methods, Doctrine, Free Methodist Catechism and Discipline, Church History, Bible, Geography, Music, Hygiene and Home-Making. There are two Chinese women teachers besides the missionaries. The students come to this school from far and near. Some are wives of the Men's Bible School students. Some are daughters of our pastors. A spiritual atmosphere prevails. Much of the success is due to the faithfulness of the principal—Miss Wood.

Miss Jones is our senior missionary in China, having given faithful service for twenty-seven years. At her own request she is taking her furlough in her beloved China.

1934 statistics show: Missionaries, 23; stations with resident missionaries, 6; outstations, 21; organized churches, 20; members in full connection, 616; members on probation, 233; Sunday-schools, 23; officers and members, 1,846; native contributions, $1,122.81; value of mission property, $63,600.00.

CHAPTER VII
DOMINICAN REPUBLIC

MAP OF OUR MISSION STATIONS BY GEORGE W. MILLS

CHAPTER VII

DOMINICAN REPUBLIC

1889-1895

	Began Service	Left	Died
Samuel E. Mills	November, 1889		1913
Abbie Mills	" "		1909
Esther D. Clark	August 1893	1924	

THE Dominican Republic, also called Santo Domingo, is a part of the island of Haiti, of the West Indies. It occupies about two-thirds of the eastern part of the island. Two mountain ranges extend across the country. The Free Methodist territory lies between the two, with a portion on the northern coast. Santo Domingo City, the capital, is about 1,700 miles from New York City. Roman Catholicism in a corrupt form is the prevailing religion.

Samuel E. Mills, a prosperous business man of Ashtabula, Ohio, having heard the great need of the gospel on this island, decided to answer the call. In 1889 he, with his wife and two small children, sailed for their chosen field. They spent two years in Monte Cristo, a port city. Then they moved to Santiago, where they began a noble pioneer work throughout the Cibao Valley.

In 1893 Esther D. Clark, being acquainted with Mr. and Mrs. Mills, responded to their call for help. She taught in the mission school and read the Bible from house to house. The Board gave her an occasional allowance, but no salary.

1895-1905

After laboring six years, Miss Clark returned home in 1899, but after a stay of five years again sailed for the field in 1904.

In the meantime Mr. and Mrs. Mills toiled on as faith missionaries, never receiving any support from our Board.

1905-1915

	Began Service	Left	Died
J. W. Winans	November, 1907		1932
Nellie Whiffen, R. N.	June 1908		
Wm. C. Willing. M. D.	" "	1909	
R. E. Nichols and wife	"	1910	
E. H. Stayt and wife	1912	1916	
Ethel Newton	1913	1915	

In 1907 Rev. B. Winget, the Missionary Secretary, and his wife visited this work. This was done at the urgent request of Miss Clark, but rather against the judgment of Mr. Mills. After holding a ten-days' meeting and calling upon the converts in their homes, they were impressed that this was a promising field. On the recommendation of the Missionary Secretary, the Board authorized the organization of the work. Hence in 1908, after nearly twenty years of pioneering, the mission in the Dominican Republic was established.

Mr. and Mrs. Nichols returned home on account of impaired health.

M. GRACE MURRAY

EDITH FRANCES JONES AND LORA

In 1909 Mrs. Mills finished her life work, and
in 1913 Mr. Mills joined her in death. They were
self-denying, humble and zealous workers in the
Lord's vineyard. A fine monument in Santiago
marks the resting-place of these pioneers and their
little Bennie.

1915-1925

	Began Service	Left	Died
Raul G. Leon	1915	1922	
S. Belle Avery	"	1923	
George W. Mills November,	1917		
Ruth Peverill Mills "	"		
Leslie E. Hendren	1920	1921	
Evelyn Webb Hendren	"		1921
Clara M. Hayden	"		1926
Duane Avery	"	1926	
Eva Whiffen	1921		
Harry F. Johnson September,	"	1932	
Pearl Vennard Johnson "	"	"	
Wesley O. Smith October	1923	1926	
Alice Mills Smith "	"	"	

Through the labors and prayers of those on the
field and friends at home, a church was built at
San Francisco de Macoris—the first Protestant
Spanish-speaking church in the interior. Rev. B.
Winget by request dedicated the edifice in 1915.
This was the cause of much rejoicing. Many of
the converts formerly attached to Mr. Mills' work
were glad now to find a home among the Free
Methodists with the hope of needed help and
supervision.

In 1915 a mission home and school building also

were erected at Macoris. At this time Miss Clark returned for a third term of service. Mr. and Mrs. Stayt returned home because of his father's illness.

The coming of G. W. Mills, son of the pioneer, and his wife was a happy occasion for the missionaries. Mr. Mills as a child had acquired the use of the Spanish language, and his understanding of the native people greatly increased his usefulness.

These new recruits gave their time mostly to the school work. Here the Bible, English, music and household science were given an important place in the curriculum. This school, known as the San Francisco de Macoris Lincoln School, was the only Protestant boarding school in the country. Its influence extended into many Roman Catholic homes.

In 1919 a general meeting of the missionaries and converts under the leadership of J. W. Winans was held at Santiago. This took place during holy week, when a large number from the surrounding country would be present. From a report of the gathering we quote the following:

Sixty-five persons partook of the Lord's Supper. It was the first time the new communion set was used. Sixteen persons joined the church in full connection. The gospel seems to have come to stay in the Dominican Republic. Prejudice is wearing away.

In February, 1921, the Missionary Secretary, Rev. W. B. Olmstead, and his wife visited the most important points on the island and dedicated the new church at Sanchez. At this time, Miss Eva L. Whiffen, who had labored here several years with her sister, came under the Board as a regular missionary.

An opportunity also came to rent a large hotel building which had recently been vacated. Thus an auditorium and rooms for all the Santiago missionaries, and within one block of the center of the city, were provided.

In March of that year, Melba Marie Hendren, the three-year-old daughter of Rev. and Mrs. Hendren, died of cerebro-spinal meningitis. She was known as "Everybody's Baby."

Just three months later the mother died at San Francisco de Macoris, of a relapse following typhoid fever. Her life was one of uplifting service. Her last public work was in her English Sunday-school. In the autumn Mr. Hendren and the nine-months'-old baby boy returned to California.

Mr. and Mrs. Johnson in writing of first impressions said:

There are no two missionaries anywhere near alike, yet they agree and a spirit of cooperation exists. If an unbelieving world wants to know of the virtues of Christianity, we call them to notice the heroic efforts, the unselfish devotion, and the uncomplaining spirit of those who labor here.

The school, which had been closed for a year, was opened again; but owing to the financial depression and the political situation, the attendance was small. Then an epidemic of smallpox caused mission work to be practically at a standstill for some time.

Again in 1922 Rev. W. B. Olmstead and wife visited the island, en route from Panama. Many problems were waiting to be solved. Rev. G. W. Mills was made superintendent in the absence of

J. W. Winans on furlough. Many meetings were held in different sections which were a great spiritual impetus to the church. This was followed by a revival all over the field. Later a large tent was secured and used in various parts of the island. All this helped to break down prejudice. It was the beginning of ten years' reaping time.

The Young Men's Seminary was located at Santiago, the largest city in our territory. Rev. H. F. Johnson was made principal, with his wife as assistant. A building in the center of the city that for a long time they had hoped to secure was purchased for $6,000.00.

It also was decided to enter La Vega, an important city thirty miles southeast of Santiago. This town was a rich, intellectual Catholic center. Miss Whiffen and her sister were chosen for this difficult task.

Maximo Conde, having been graduated from Greenville College in 1923, returned to his native island. He was the first ordained minister among his people. The following year he married a worthy helpmeet.

For Alice Mills Smith, a daughter of the early pioneer, it was a "home-going," as she was born there and was familiar with the language and life of the country. Health conditions and family obligations necessitated the return of Mr. and Mrs. Smith after a brief term of service. This was a source of grief to the missionaries.

Most of the United States marines were adventurous boys out for a good time. This situation increased the opposition to the enterprise of Chris-

tian missions. Life for the missionaries has been
easier since the marines left in 1924.

1925-1935

	Began Service		Left	Died
Mae L. Smith	January	1925	1928	
Jessie E. Ragatz	September,	1927	1930	
Rachel Smiley	"	1929		
Edmund C. Snyder	"	1931		
Clara Zahniser Snyder	"	"		

In 1926 a printing-press was purchased and Mr.
Mills began to issue a semi-monthly publication.

In July, 1926, Miss Clara Hayden, while on furlough, finished her life of service on earth and
slipped away to the better land. She was an exceptional teacher, and her unselfish spirit made a lasting impression on all with whom she labored.

In February, 1927, Rev. and Mrs. H. F. Johnson, after a furlough, returned for a second term of
service to their chosen field. Again the Missionary
Secretary visited the island. At this time the Bible
schools for men and women were united. The mission property in Santiago was sold to good advan-
tage, and two separate properties for the school and
the church were purchased. The school site consists of thirty-six acres just outside the congested
city of Santiago. This is desirable so that agriculture may be taught, for Latin-Americans need to
learn the dignity of labor. The church-lot is in
the heart of the city. The erection of the needed
buildings was put in the hands of Mr. Johnson,

who was the principal of the school and also the pastor of the church.

At the annual meeting of the missionaries, unity and Christian fellowship prevailed to a remarkable degree. The word "friction" seemed to be unknown.

In 1928, the principal of the Evangelical Institute, as the united schools were named, reported a full school. The new three-story, modern, brick structure is the home for the girls, and is known as "Hayden Hall." The building already built serves as the principal's residence and Boys' Hall.

Later in the year, the missionaries wrote:

Our school gardens are a great success. Now that the rains have come, the tomato vines are bearing a second crop. We also have corn, sweet potatoes in abundance, and other vegetables.

In a letter from Mr. Mills dated November 30, 1929, he said:

We are emerging from another one of the numerous tropical storms that we have been having this year. The whole country is flooded. Provisions are scarce and high in price, and there is much suffering among the people.

In August, 1929, Rev. J. W. Winans passed away in a hospital in Hamilton, Ontario, following an operation. He loved the poor, neglected people of the Dominican Republic, and was used of God in the salvation of many.

Early in 1930, a boys' dormitory was erected on the Santiago school property, as it was unsatisfactory for the boys to live in the building used as the home of the principal.

In 1930, while the Missionary Secretary was

again on the island, a Provisional Conference was organized. Seven pastors were ordained and the Santiago church was dedicated. There was a forward movement toward self-support.

In June, 1930, Miss Ragatz, having returned home on account of climatic conditions, was married to Mr. Herbert Booth.

Miss Mae Smith, who had taught in the Lincoln School, returned home after a term of service. Later she was married to Mr. Cecil Morris.

In 1931, in behalf of the wife's health, Mr. and Mrs. Johnson returned to the States. Mr. and Mrs. Snyder were appointed as their successors, and as soon as they were able assumed the responsibilities of the Santiago School.

The fourth annual session of the Provisional Conference was held at Santiago in April, 1933. Rev. H. F. Johnson, Missionary Secretary, but a former coworker and principal of the school, presided without need of an interpreter. The reports showed both spiritual and material progress. Native contributions had increased. Mr. Mills was chosen district elder of the entire conference.

The conference of 1934 was held by Rev. F. L. Baker. He was impressed with the poverty of the people, but was glad for the spiritual hunger that existed on every hand.

Miss Abrams, who has done most excellent work wherever appointed to labor, returned to this country in the spring of 1934, broken in health. The Great Physician touched her body, and in November joyfully she again sailed for her chosen field.

Many causes have contributed to the splendid growth and development of missions in this field.

1. Material changes. Where there were only bridle paths, now there is a network of auto roads. Large sea-going hydroplanes carrying twenty-two passengers fly down over the islands three times a week. A letter from Chicago reaches there in three days.

2. Personal contacts. By means of teaching private classes in English, Father Mills had won many influential friends. This was an entering wedge in gaining the good-will of the people. The work of the Whiffen sisters and of Miss Abrams in nursing and giving aid in multitudes of homes has been most effective.

The articles in the daily papers about the "Pernicious Protestant Institutions" have served as free advertising. The people have come to the churches and schools to learn for themselves. They are not afraid now. They ask questions and have opened their homes to the missionaries.

3. The Sunday-school. They have been an important factor. The Ford, the small folding organ, picture rolls and cards—each has had a part on the streets in gathering in the children. Santiago, no doubt, has the largest Sunday-school in the denomination. This is due in part to the indefatigable labors of Miss Nellie Whiffen and Miss Smiley.

4. Demand for Bibles. This shows the undercurrent towards Protestantism. Sixteen thousand copies of the New Testament, donated by a philanthropist, were in a few months placed in homes where the people promised to read a chapter a day. They are hungry for the Word of Life.

5. Native leadership. In 1930 when the Provisional Conference was organized, Santiago was a self-supporting church; others in part. Native ministry has given much valuable advice and information concerning management of the church. They feel the work is theirs, and they are responsible for its success or failure. General Rosario, a converted revolutionist, has done much in the western part of the territory and Mr. Conde in the eastern part as evan-

gelists. They are strong, capable workers. There are now three ordained elders and five ordained deacons on the field.

There are also many worthy women. Mrs. Mary Fawcett Payano is one. She is a remarkable woman in prayer and in securing and holding the attention of a congregation. Another is Sra. Easter Jimeney. She is a lawyer's daughter and has put many a Roman priest to flight. Still another is Sra. Aurora Mota. With a heart full of love she goes forth to share her joy with her people until they are won to Christ. There are also exhorters and Bible women not a few, who help to make up the army of faithful, tireless toilers.

An opening has appeared on the south side of the island for some of the young women converts to take training in a large Protestant hospital. Two were rapidly advanced. They were the only two chosen among many to be sent to the United States to finish their training.

Our denomination is known all over the island as the real convert and the holiness church.

The door into this beautiful southland island is wide open. The opportunity is ours.

1934 statistics show: Missionaries, 8; stations with resident missionaries, 14; outstations, 125; organized churches, 15; members in full connection, 464; members on probation, 329; Sunday-schools, 73; officers and members, 2,832; native contributions, $1,265.78; value of property, $56,258.50.

CHAPTER VIII

HOME MISSIONS

PANAMA AND THE CANAL ZONE

KENTUCKY MISSIONS

MEXICAN MISSIONS

JAPANESE HOME MISSIONS

ITALIAN MISSION

AMERICAN INDIANS

AMONG FOREIGNERS AT MASON CITY

GREEK-AMERICAN MISSION

CHAPTER VIII

HOME MISSIONS

PANAMA AND THE CANAL ZONE

THE Canal Zone is a strip of land ten miles wide, extending from the Atlantic to the Pacific, a distance of fifty miles. The canal crosses the Isthmus from northwest to southeast. It was opened to commerce in August, 1915.

The population consists of Negroes and the Panamanians, who are a mixture of Spanish, Indian and Chinese.

Here our first venture in Home Missions began. Mr. S. N. House of St. Louis, having spent the winter there, became impressed with the spiritual needs of the people. He wrote stirring appeals to the Missionary Secretary, Rev. B. Winget. Providentially Mr. F. W. Amsden, a member of the Free Methodist Church from New York, was in the Canal Zone at that time in the employ of the government. The Missionary Board engaged him to give part time to the work.

The following have served this field during the quarter of a century:

	Began Service	Left	Died
F. W. Amsden	1910	1922	
B. L. Beegle	1922	1926	
Gladys Smith Beegle	1922	1926	
Emma Corson (Pearson)	1922	1924	

A. M. Anderson	1929	1929
Mary Damon Anderson	1929	1929
Florence Hilborn	1930	
Elaine Hilborn	1930	1933

Under the direction of the Board, Mr. Amsden purchased the site now occupied in Panama City. This city is at the Pacific end of the canal and just outside of the Zone, hence in the Panama Republic.

Six miles away, but in the Canal Zone, is Red Tank, a colored settlement, where another mission was located.

In 1918 Mr. Amsden wrote:

There is a good school at each place. We work in the prison and hospital and on the street.

Panama is a place of bull-fights, red-lights, rum and Romanism.

We have had scores of souls decide for Christ, but the trouble is to keep them. The temptations are so great. There is much deprivation and hunger.

In 1920 Rev. and Mrs. F. L. Baker visited this field under the direction of the Board. Mrs. Baker wrote:

This field seems to be harder than in heathen countries. Brother Amsden is a very self-sacrificing man. He has put all he has earned while working for the government into this work. We plan to visit every home in this section.

Many English-speaking colored people came from the British West Indies to Panama to obtain work during the construction of the canal. Our labors have been largely among these people. Very little provision has been made by the Republic of Panama for the education of the colored children. The school opened by our workers was a great asset.

Brother Baker wrote:

After the dedication of the new church, the school was removed to the new quarters. The pupils in line, led by the teacher, marched to the new church, singing with all their might, "We're Marching to Zion," and when seated in their new room, sang, with shining faces, "I've Reached the Land of Corn and Wine." Brother Boise, our native teacher, is said to be one of the best teachers among his race in Panama City.

The strenuous labors of Brother Baker in that trying climate subjected him to typhoid fever and he was obliged to return home at once. He and Mrs. Baker gladly would have spent their remaining years there.

Mr. Alleyne, a native pastor, working under the direction of Brother Amsden, proved to be very efficient. After his fatal accident, Mr. C. M. Sealey was secured as a native evangelist and pastor.

In the spring of 1922, the Missionary Secretary, Rev. W. B. Olmstead, and his wife visited Panama, taking with them the three new missionaries. At this time the parsonage was screened with copper screening. This protection from mosquitoes and other pests was much appreciated by the missionaries.

In a letter from Mrs. Beegle we quote:

How thankful we were for the church bell. Now we are able to announce to the surrounding community our services. It looks as though we would have to have more seats before long.

The street organ is a great asset to the open-air services. Many are impressed with the messages of truth which they hear. Often a holy quietness comes over all. We have many heart-stirring scenes.

Then the motor wheel for the colored pastor is a great help. Also the box of new song books and papers from

the Publishing House was greatly needed and appreciated.
Each person to whom a book is given feels the responsi-
bility of caring for it. We are very anxious to master the
Spanish language.

Again from Mrs. Beegle in 1924:

We had a joyous Christmas season. But it seems un-
natural to look out on the landscape so green and beautiful.
A great many of our friends came in during the day to
greet us. The missionaries and children had a very happy
time opening the many packages sent by friends and
relatives.

The church at Red Tank has been made almost new by
needed repairs. With the two carpenters Mr. Beegle stayed
on the job in spite of the heat.

We began a revival last night and four seekers prayed
through to victory. We feel our helplessness as never
before. At times the people seem so indifferent and appear
to be seeking material aid instead of spiritual. Continue
to pray for us.

The three missionaries sent in 1922 proved to be
most valuable laborers, but climatic conditions compelled each to return to the states.

Mrs. Anna R. Dresselhaus, a member of the Free
Methodist Church in Los Angeles, but a resident of
the Canal Zone while her husband was in government employ, wrote:

The fifth anniversary service of the dedication of our
church in Panama City was held November 25, 1925. The
building was packed to its capacity. Brother Sealey led
the testimony meeting. Not one referred to a trial or hard-
ship. Many of their faces shone with divine light. Seventy partook of the sacrament.

In 1927 the Secretary again visited the field, taking with him Rev. and Mrs. Johnson, who were
returning to the Dominican Republic. At that time

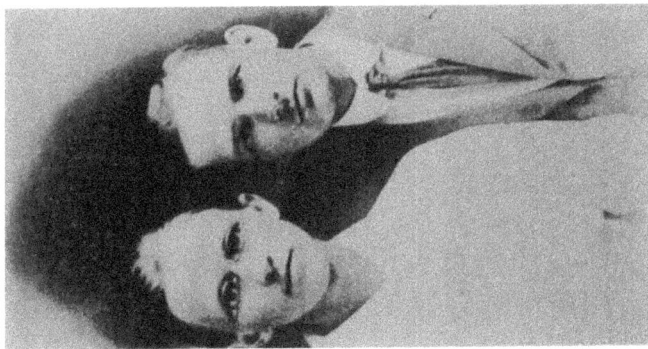

REV. AND MRS. GEORGE W. MILLS

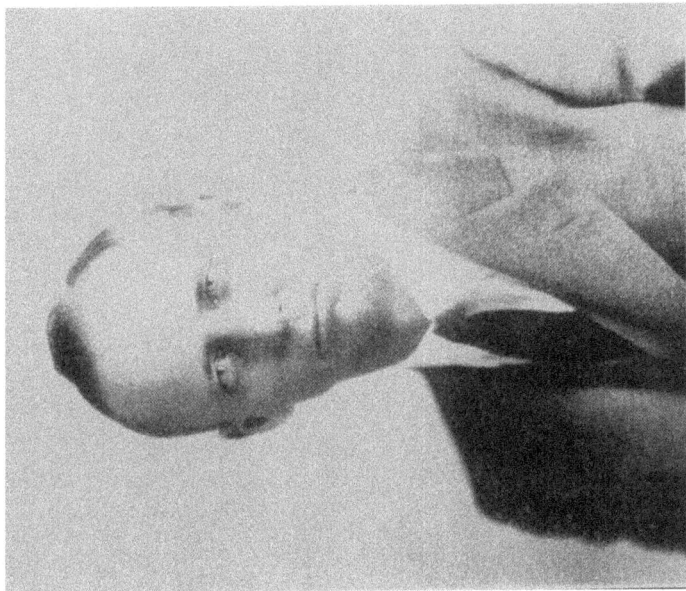

REV. H. F. JOHNSON

NELLIE WHIFFEN AND WORKER

ELIZABETH O'CONNOR

REV. AND MRS. CLYDE BURNETT

the Panama work was put on a self-supporting basis with the exception of Rev. Mr. Sealey's salary.

Mr. Anderson in writing of first impressions said:

The multitudes in Panama City hustle and bustle like a Chicago market street. Another thing was the extremely clean-looking appearance of everybody, high or low, rich or poor.

The spirit of the believers makes us feel at home. We sense that God dwells among His people here just as He does in Africa and in the States.

Later from Mrs. Anderson:

In February the first anniversary of the W. M. S. organization was celebrated. There was a crowded house and a liberal offering was received.

Again the Secretary went to Panama in 1930.

Miss Hilborn soon reported several Spanish converts. One Spanish meeting a week was planned for each week.

The Hilborn sisters, who seemed so well qualified for service, on account of health were compelled to return to the States.

Since the Hilborn sisters left, the native converts have been carrying on the work unaided. In February, 1935, Senor Avila and family set sail for this field. It was a real sacrifice for the Mexican Provisional Conference in Southern California to consent to this, but they did and also agreed to pay his salary from their own budget. This family know the Spanish language and are acclimated to the tropics.

May success attend the labors of those who toil for us at this Crossroads of the World.

KENTUCKY MISSIONS

In the fall of 1914 a small three-room shack was built on what is now the site of the mission home at Oakdale, Kentucky, in Breathitt County. It was very roughly constructed, and when the lumber seasoned, large cracks were in the wall and floor, making it a very cold place when the thermometer registered zero.

"Who is that stranger?" "Why is she here?" These were some of the questions asked among the neighbors concerning our first worker, Miss Marian Eason. They soon learned why she was in their midst. The sick mothers, the children, and even the strong, husky men came for treatment when something was wrong physically. The little home became a hospital, and through this avenue of service the gospel message was given and the Holy Spirit began to work on hearts.

The first convert was the father of a large family. After he was saved one could hear the voice of prayer coming from the little home as one passed the roadside. He was having family prayer with the children around the hearth-stone.

The first Sunday-school was organized in the kitchen of the Mission Home, with four scholars. Out of this small acorn we have now a large oak, spreading its branches in all directions, north, south, east, and west. Let us look at these branches.

At Oakdale we have the church and the school. The former was organized in January of 1920. Since that time the work has been known as a Free Methodist work. There were at Oakdale thirty-five probationers. The conference claims are met every year. In 1933-34 the Woman's Missionary Society raised $58.00 and the Y. P. M. S. $23.00. If one had visited the place some twenty years ago, and then had the privilege of going back now, it would be a change like night and day. As one gets off the train at Oakdale station and walks up the track for half a mile, he will be told by the mountain people that that big building in the valley is Oakdale Vocational School. It is a splendid building four stories high, including a dormitory for girls, classrooms which can be made into a large auditorium, a library consisting of over 1,500 books, a dining-room, a kitchen, pantry, weaving department, laundry, and a furnace and a coal room. In this building, sixty high school students meet daily for classes. As it is a mission school, they must pay tuition. The following are a list of some of the things brought on tuition: Corn, coal, sorghum, vegetables of all kinds, chickens, butter, milk, and anything that the missionary may need.

The next twig on the Oakdale Branch is the Manual Training building. In this the high school boys are taught to make furniture of all kinds. You ask, "How do they do it?" We can not tell. It is like getting saved. They do it and we can not tell you just how. Trees are cut down in the woods, they are sawed at the mill, planed by hand quite often, seasoned out and brought to the shop for tables or chairs, or perhaps for a desk or a bed, whatever the project may be. The second floor of this building is used for a dwelling apartment by one of the married couples.

Turn now to the building at the south end of the campus. It is the most sacred. It is the church. In it many souls have sought and found God. Shouts of praise and victory have been heard during the last thirteen years within its walls. At present, during the week days it is used as a music hall. The piano is in the back of the building and has a covering over it during service. In the basement of the church, the expense of which was partly covered through the relief fund some two years ago, the first six grades of the school are taught.

The one other division on the Oakdale branch is rather a new one. It is the Home Art Cottage. The High Sheriff of Jackson donated a fallen-down building, one which had good lumber in it, and out of this was built the framework of the Home Art Cottage. The roof is made of hand-made, wooden shingles. The weather-boarding was made at the country mills. Part of the walls inside are felt paper and others are carton boxes. Over the latter is wallpaper. The inside finishing of this building is being done by the students of the Home Economics Class of the high school. They are making it look like a little palace. The wall-paper was donated by different missionary societies. In this building five workers are living. As there are not enough beds, springs and mattresses are placed on heavy logs of wood, and the teachers have a good bed.

The next branch on this great oak is Rock Lick, five miles from Oakdale. There is a fine church building and a four-room parsonage. Brother John Riley and wife and little David live there. How do you think they get the milk for David? Funds were low, very much so; and they could not buy a cow. David's mother while in prayer one day told Jesus all about the matter of milk for the little boy. He gave her that promise in Proverbs 27:27, "And thou shalt have goat's milk enough for thy food, for the food of thy household."

She told her husband that the Lord was going to send them some goats. A letter came from a dear saint in McPherson, Kansas, asking if they could use some goats. The goats came and it caused some excitement when the news spread that Miss O'Connor had goats.

Then there is a branch at Athol and two workers living in part of the church partitioned off. At Jackson there is another and a married couple stationed at that point, and effort is being made to establish Free Methodism in the county seat of Breathitt County.

In another direction is the Curt branch. Here are Brother Oral Drew and wife and two children, also the school teacher, Miss Ruth Whitehead. When Mr. Drew went to this field he was told to start the building—a home to live in and a church. There was not a piece of lumber on the grounds. That very afternoon he started the work by cutting logs on the high hills. Now there is a good church building in which they teach school, and a home consisting of five rooms, not all finished.

The Elkatawa branch is the last one which has cropped out of this tree. They are using a community church for services. The worker is Miss Georgia Babcock, a trained nurse and preacher combined. Rev. Alex. Wilson, our native preacher, is the pastor. Recently during a revival several parents sought the Lord.

The name of Miss Elizabeth O'Connor is closely linked with the story of Kentucky missions. Through the years she has proved to be the right woman for the place. Miss Mildred Norbeck and Miss Myrtle Anderson for several years have been efficient helpers in the church and school work. More than a score of others, several of whom are college graduates, are sharing in the sacrifices common to this field. All this portends a great future for the Free Methodist Church in the mountains.

MEXICAN MISSIONS

Free Methodist Mexican missions began in the heart-cry of two consecrated members of the Woman's Missionary Society. Mrs. Emma F. Shay and Mrs. Elizabeth Wyatt looked out upon the half million Mexican population of Southern California and were constrained to pray the Lord of the harvest to send forth laborers into His harvest. Faith laid hold of the promise, and they held steady until God's plans were matured.

At a great revival meeting in the Hermon Free Methodist Church, Los Angeles, California, prayer, power and faith came to a splendid group of young people, and on February 23, 1917, B. H. Pearson was converted.

Fired with the Holy Spirit's presence, this group of young people whom God had used in the revival were ready to follow "the Man with the nail-pierced hands." Mrs. Elizabeth Wyatt, and Mrs. Clara R.

Freeland, who for so many years was identified with the home missions work as treasurer of the Executive Committee in Southern California, rented the first Mexican mission at 108 Sotello Street, Los Angeles. On April 18, 1917, the first street-meetings were held, and a noisy mob of children filled the basement hall which for a number of years was headquarters for the work. The great initial step had been taken. Something had been STARTED! Prayer was being answered.

Miss Nella True resigned her position in a bank to accept appointment as the first superintendent of the mission. A group from the Hermon revival assisted her. Her faithful sister, Ethel, was her constant companion in the work. By December, 1918, there were eleven members; in 1919, twenty-four members; and this group has grown until today there are over 150 members in a self-supporting church at 1510 North Main Street, Los Angeles, less than half a block from where the work began. A property at Chino, California, was purchased May 27, 1919, and in 1920 five members were reported.

In August, 1920, an old boathouse was purchased at Terminal Island. The prayers and personal activity of Mrs. Phoebe Langdon were responsible for opening this work. Brother and Sister Cisneros, converts at the Chino Mission, were called to assume the responsibilities of this difficult charge. The building was later moved over to the mainland at Wilmington, California, where it now houses the church and Sunday-school. At Palo Verde, near Elysian Park, Los Angeles, a lot was purchased and tent-meetings were held in a large Mexican community in June, 1922. A mission building was later erected, and on February 17, 1924, the society was organized with thirteen members.

Miss Lela Roll became interested in the Mexican Colony in the West End of Santa Ana, California, in the year 1922, and held an open-air Sunday-school for them for over a year. She secured a Mexican preacher by working in a laundry. Brother and Sister Cisneros went there. Due to Miss Roll's efforts a property and a fine mission building were secured without expense to the Board. On February 10, 1924, a society was organized with eleven members.

The Mexican Girls' Training Home was begun through the sacrificial efforts of Miss Ruth Kenworthy, who was its founder and first matron. This work was successfully continued by Mrs. Adelaide L. Beers, who has served so faithfully for nine years in this field, not only in the Girls' Home but as matron of the Mexican Boys' Training Home and as missionary in Mexico.

Prior to 1924 the individual Mexican circuits were reported as home mission societies in districts of the Southern California Conference. In April of that year the conference formed according to the Discipline a Mexican Home Mission District. Deepest gratitude is due the Southern California Conference by all who are interested in Mexican missions for establishing and supporting this work during the early years. The General Missionary Board assumed responsibility for continuing these missions upon condition that the conference would continue its interest and contributions toward them.

Without the cooperation, prayers, encouragement, financial backing, and hard work in erecting buildings which came from the people of Southern California, particularly from Rev. and Mrs. W. W. Vinson, Mr. and Mrs. A. G. Ball, Mrs. Clara R. Freeland, Rev. George B. French, and others, this work would have been impossible.

In 1924 property was purchased at 1510 North Main Street, Los Angeles, and the following year a two-story brick building was erected which has since housed the Hahnemann Medical and Surgical Clinic, the local congregation and Sunday-school, and the home mission headquarters.

The work of the Hahnemann Medical and Surgical Clinic, Inc., was begun in a very informal way by our missionaries in the year 1919. Now it serves over 5,000 patients a year, and is still growing. A full-time missionary seeks to convert the many contacts made here into spiritual values.

Following 1924 there came in quick succession the establishment of missions at Belvedere of Maraville Park (the "Floral Drive Mission" of Belvedere, Los Angeles), Richfield or Atwood, all of California, and of Chandler in Arizona. Each of these has a story of its own.

But while this development was going forward in the United States, a movement was gathering momentum which overshadowed all of this—the prospect of entrance into Mexico. At the Mexican Woman's Missionary Society Convention at Chino, California, in November, 1928, Miss Minerva Quesada gave an address on Sonora, Mexico, which moved all hearts to prayer.

In an effort to find an open door in Mexico, in September, 1929, B. H. Pearson and Emeterio Soto were sent on a trip through that land with money coming from the Mexican people. Later, the Missionary Secretary, Rev. W. B. Olmstead, and B. H. Pearson went into the northern part of Sonora. It seemed that God was calling us that way. Brother Cisneros had always felt the call of God to go as a minister to his own native State of Sonora. Other doors closed. Through Bishop Juan Nicanor Pascoe of the Methodist Church of Mexico arrangements were made whereby the Free Methodist Church became responsible for the evangelization of the northern part of Sonora. In the First Mexican Conference, which was organized by the Missionary Secretary, Rev. W. B. Olmstead, at Chino, California, on Thanksgiving Day, 1931, Brother and Sister Cisneros and two missionaries, Miss Candida Molina and Miss Micaela Saavedra, were appointed for Mexico. The work in Mexico could never have been begun except for a cash contribution of $1,000 made by Mr. and Mrs. Wesley Crawford of Tacoma, Washington.

God blessed and prospered the work in Sonora, and the last report showed 330 Free Methodists in Mexico. There is a greatly-disturbed politico-religious situation in this Southern land, as they are attempting to eliminate superstition and a religious tyranny which in the past they feel has retarded national development. As this is being written, October, 1934, several of our churches have been taken possession of by the radical labor groups and as a result preachers and people are carrying forward the task of evangelization in the homes. A great Gospel Distribution Campaign is under way, by which it is hoped through the Christians to place in the hands of every individual who will accept it a copy of the special Personal Worker's Edition of the Gospel of John in Spanish. A real attempt is being made to see people converted. Many thousands are being reached in this way who were entirely untouched before. Cities and towns and villages which we might not have evangelized for years are now gladly receiving the precious Word of God. Twenty thousand Gospels have been shipped to Mexico for distribution, and 100,000 more are needed. Mexico greatly needs the prayers of God's children that she may be able to achieve true independence, political liberty, freedom of conscience and religious worship.

One of God's gifts to the Mexican Provisional Conference is the large theater building located at 4232 Floral Drive, Los Angeles, California, where the annual conferences and missionary conventions are held. This building, valued at $10,000.00, seats approximately four hundred people and was acquired through exchange without any special appropriation from the Missionary Board. To visit the general gatherings, see the altars filled with earnest seekers, sense the deep burden of prayer, and hear, though perhaps not understand, the testimonies of men and women saved and cleansed by the precious blood of Christ, is better to understand what answered prayer has meant and is meaning to the Mexican Missions.

1934 statistics show: Missionaries, American, 5; Mexican men ordained, 10; Mexican men, evangelists, not ordained, 9; women workers, including Bible women, 7; organized churches, 15; members in full connection, 554; members on probation, 85; Sunday-schools, 14; officers and members, 81; native contributions, $2,272.20; value of mission property: value of land, $17,550.00; value of buildings, $40,850.00.

JAPANESE HOME MISSIONS

In the autumn of 1915, Miss Lillian Pool, a missionary who had returned from Japan on account of ill health, felt a great burden for the Japanese people in the bay district of San Francisco. She sold her piano in order to secure a ticket to Berkeley, California. Being a member of the Nazarene Church, she taught English and organized a Sunday-school among the Japanese people for that church. God blessed the effort and some were saved.

Later when the Nazarene Church decided to give up their home mission work among the Japanese people, Miss Pool prayed for guidance as to where she should take her church and people. In the providence of God she came in contact with Rev. Alexander Beers and Rev. J. A. Barnhart, elders in the North California Conference of the Free Methodist Church. She told them her desire to come into the Free Methodist Church and bring her Japanese people with her. In due time the change was made and the church with a membership of sixteen became the Japanese Free Methodist Church of Berkeley. Miss Pool served faithfully for eight years in the work at Berkeley as missionary and pastor. Those assisting her were Mr. Misawa, who was a very efficient pastor, but later went to Japan and engaged in pastoral work there. Mr. Tomiki, who was converted under her labors, is now serving one of the churches in Japan. Mr. Yamamoto, who also was converted and studied for the ministry and later became pastor of the church in Berkeley, died after two years of successful pastoral work. Mr. Nishimura was converted as a young man and was graduated from the Nampa Nazarene College and later from the University of California, and is now the efficient pastor of the church at Berkeley. Rev. A. Youngren has rendered splendid work among the Japanese of Northern California, being for a number of years appointed superintendent by the General Missionary Board.

Miss Pool, after eight years of missionary work in Berkeley, decided to enter the Bible Institute of Los Angeles. Here she spent two years in Bible study and preparation, assisting in the Japanese work in Anaheim. At the end of two years she was united in marriage to Rev. Clyde J. Burnett, pastor of the Free Methodist Church in Santa Monica. During their pastorate in this city, they became interested in the unevangelized Japanese people in Santa Monica and vicinity and began active work among them. At the close of the two-years' pastorate, they decided to engage exclusively in Japanese work. Under their labors the work in Santa Monica grew and developed. A church building was purchased for a Japanese church, and later a parsonage and Sunday-school rooms were erected on the rear of the church lot. A number of Japanese people have been saved and are now organized into a Free Methodist church. During their mission work in Santa Monica, Rev. Mr. Burnett was appointed by the General Missionary Board as superintendent of the Japanese Home Missions, which place he has been filling for the past four years.

The work in Anaheim was begun under the labors of Rev. Mr. Miyabe, assisted by Rev. A. Youngren. A small society was organized and a five-room house was built for a parsonage and church work. Eight years ago Rev. Mr. Shigekawa was appointed pastor of this church and, under his faithful labors, the work has grown and prospered until now it is one of the strongest churches. Four years ago, because of the growing Sunday-school and church, it was necessary to build a new church building at Anaheim and, under the blessing of the Lord, a commodious church building was erected and dedicated to the work of God.

In 1919, Mrs. Elizabeth Wyatt and other members of the Woman's Missionary Society became burdened for the thousands of Japanese living in Los Angeles. With the cooperation of Mrs. Maude Thornton, who had spent several years in Japan as a missionary, and Mr. Mezukami, an ordained elder, they set out in search of a suitable location.

A spacious room was decided upon and soon made habitable. This was situated near several heathen temples. But despite opposition the place was soon filled with children.

Soon services for adults were started and although the Japanese helper had but little experience as a preacher, the story of his wonderful conversion, related by himself time and again, led many to seek the Christ of Christianity.

The corps of workers was increased. Numerous day classes and a night school for the teaching of English were conducted.

In those early days the marvelous grace of God was manifested in many ways. On one occasion a worker was called to see a young woman who was enduring great suffering. God saved her soul and healed her body. She went from house to house testifying to God's love, and won many trophies for Christ.

A young newspaper man who had been seriously ill was converted. He developed a love for God's Word, reading the New Testament through twice in one week. Later he died triumphantly.

Another transformation was that of a young dentist, who had come to America for study. One Sunday he was asked to attend our Sunday-school. After listening to the lesson story of Christ in Gethsemane, he became an earnest inquirer. After a fearful struggle the power of Satan was at last broken and he became a mighty witness to the power of God to save.

The Missionary Board assisted in securing a permanent building. Los Angeles Pacific College maintained a successful night school program for them, and Rev. A. Youngren also ably assisted.

Some who were Juniors in the Sunday-school in those early days are now married and bringing their little ones to church. Not a few are preaching the gospel in this land and in far-away Japan.

The superintendent, Rev. Clyde J. Burnett, was

called to Phoenix, Arizona, three years ago to take
charge of a new Sunday-school which was being
superintended by a Japanese man, Mr. Uyema.
After a year and a half of earnest work, assisted by
different Japanese ministers and by Mrs. Burnett,
the work grew and it became necessary to buy property and erect our own church building. One of
our members, Mr. Sagawa, a farmer in Phoenix,
drew $1,500 from his savings account and made the
cash payment on the seven acres of land purchased.
The Lord marvelously blessed in the erection of the
church building, and in a very short time the building was completed and dedicated to the worship of
God. It seemed, after much prayer and consultation,
that a provisional conference should be organized,
which would cover the states of California and
Arizona. This conference was organized by Rev.
W. B. Olmstead by order of the General Missionary
Board, at Anaheim, California, November 11-13,
1932. God has very graciously put His seal upon
the organizing of the conference, and the growth
has been steady and substantial. At the present
time there is a total membership of 207.

Three wonderful camp-meetings have been held
at the Pacific Palisades, California. God signally
owned with His presence and power the first, which
was held in 1932. Many souls were converted and
the light of the gospel was brought to many new
people. The one in 1934 was the climax of all, the
attendance being much larger than in previous years,
and the power of God was wonderfully manifested
in the saving of souls and the sanctifying of believers. A conference Y. P. M. S. was organized in

REV. AND MRS. B. H. PEARSON AND DAUGHTER

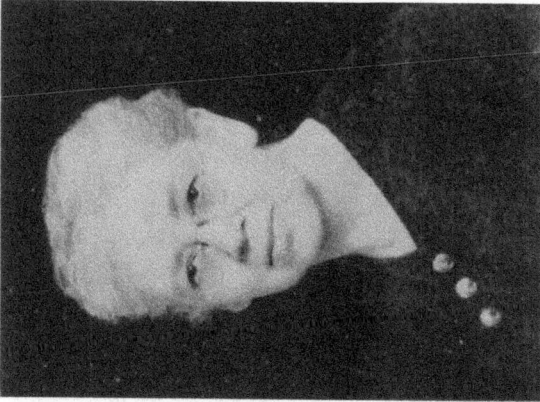

CARRIE T. BURRITT

MARY L. COLEMAN

1933 with one hundred members, and this year they reported a gain in membership of twenty-five.

There are eleven Sunday-schools in the conference, which reach between five and six hundred children and young people each Sunday. The Y. P. M. S. and Junior Societies are spiritual and aggressive. The fields are white unto harvest.

ITALIAN MISSION

It was the last Sunday in June, 1924. The attendance at the Melrose Park, Illinois, Free Methodist Sunday-school was smaller than usual. Many were attending the Glen Ellyn camp-meeting. But the superintendent and pastor found some bright-eyed, dark-haired Italian boys present that morning. During the previous week an eager Italian mother had called at the parsonage, soliciting the pastor's interest in the Italian families of the town. He welcomed her and asked her to send the children to Sunday-school, and there they were!

They continued to come regularly and brought other boys and girls. Sometimes the fathers and mothers came bringing babies in their arms. Soon they were found at other services. Often they were outside waiting for the door to open. They came in all sorts of weather, though the church was quite a distance from their quarter of the town. They entered into the spirit of the services, and many responded to the call of the Holy Spirit and found peace in believing.

This was a new avenue for service for the Melrose Park church. The pastor, Rev. S. V. Kline, found a welcome as he went to call and pray in these Italian homes. As the months went by, the need of a place for worship in their own community became evident. There were two thousand Italian citizens in Melrose Park. They would not attend the Free Methodist Church, but they might be reached if a mission were opened near them.

In October, 1924, the Missionary Board appointed Mr. Kline superintendent and granted an appropriation. A hall was rented for services but soon had to be discontinued as the rent was excessive. Meetings were held in the homes, but a permanent place for worship was desired. The way opened. A store building adapted to the mission needs was purchased and moved to a desirable location. Needed alterations and repairs were soon made. In supervising and directing the project, Mr. Kline gave of his time and labor unstintingly.

In May, 1925, the mission became a reality and was formally opened. Rev. W. B. Olmstead used as a text, "Be Strong." Mr. Previte interpreted. At this service nearly $2,000, representing half of the indebtedness, was pledged.

The following month Angelo Previte, having been graduated from Greenville College, became pastor of the mission. Soon a course in manual training, with Bible study at the close of the hour, was started. The Child Welfare Association held a baby clinic at the mission one day each week. The mission cooperated in the Daily Vacation Bible School.

In 1927 Rev. George E. Kline was appointed superintendent and acted in that capacity so long as he was pastor of the local Free Methodist church.

In 1929 Rev. Newton W. Fink was appointed by the Missionary Board as superintendent, continuing for three years.

After some years of faithful ministry, Rev. Angelo Previte returned to his home conference in the east. Inquiry among the Protestant Italians of Chicago brought the superintendent in touch with Mr. Anton Traina, who became the pastor. He lived in the comfortable quarters provided in the mission building and supported his family by his daily work in the city.

Increasingly the younger people among the Italians, those who had attended the public schools, desired to have English services in the mission. In 1934, Rev. Simon V. Kline, who had been re-appointed superintendent two years before, assumed the pastorate himself. This was very acceptable to the Italians, members and friends of the mission. Rapid advancement is seen in the work. Young people are being converted and take the Bible way with enthusiasm. One young man has been sent to Spring Arbor Seminary to prepare for definite Christian service. The prospects are bright for a convincing testimony among the many thousands of Catholic Italians in Melrose Park.

AMERICAN INDIANS IN NEW MEXICO

In the year 1929, Rev. C. R. Volgamore and family were living in Gallup. One afternoon some Indians were playing ball across from their home, and as it began to rain Mrs. Hannah Brown, who was living in the Volgamore home, invited one of the Indian women in and began to talk to her. She became quite interested. About the same time Mr. Volgamore, while selling fruit and vegetables among the Indians who lived in a little village near the Santa Fe shops, sang songs and talked to them. One of the girls became so interested that she went to the Volgamore home to get a copy of the song, "Jesus Loves Me." A little later the Volgamores were invited into one of these homes for a service. From fifteen to twenty young people attended the services regularly, and learned the songs and Bible verses. Miss Anna Coop helped in organizing the work.

In the year 1930 Miss Beryl Manyon was sent as a helper and the following year was appointed by the Colorado Conference as missionary among the Indians. Mr. Volgamore and his family, who were living here at the time, continued to do all they could to assist in the work. Mr. Volgamore was appointed to this field by the conference until the year 1931.

During the past year there have been many changes; nearly all of the older children have gone away to school and are here only a month or two during the summer, and also a number of the families have moved away. But the work has gone on and has been far-reaching. Nearly all of the Indian villages east of Gallup have been reached. From fifteen to forty people have at different times sought the Lord in services held there. Many lives have been changed. They are gradually giving up their old Indian customs and superstitions and there is a very definite reaching out after God. They are strong believers in prayer, and Indians many miles away will send word to our mission asking to be prayed for, especially when they are sick.

Each year a car-load of Indians attend our district camp-meeting and they are always among the first ones to go to the altar. When they pray through they are among our best altar workers. Recently three were converted and joined the church.

This work is situated right in the very heart of a large Indian settlement consisting of about forty-five thousand Navajo Indians, and two or three thousand Pueblos. There is no other holiness church working among them. If there ever was a field "white unto the harvest," surely it is this great Southwest country.

AMERICAN INDIANS IN ONTARIO

Julia Smart (Grey), a Mohawk Indian, worked as missionary for several years among the Indians in Belleville and Alderville, Ontario. Her efforts were not in vain, as quite a number were converted under her labors.

AMONG FOREIGNERS IN MASON CITY, IOWA

In 1925, when Miss Ida O. Helgen was sent as pastor to Mason City, Iowa, she felt a great burden and began to look about to discover the special work for which the Lord had sent her to that place. She soon found that a large proportion of the population was foreign and sensed the deplorable condition among them and other neglected classes. She seemed to hear a voice saying to her, "This is your field," and during the next two years of her pastorate she engaged in jail work, visited from house to house among many nationalities and held open-air meetings. Two Summer Bible Schools were held in which much truth was planted in young hearts.

The next year Miss Helgen was appointed full-time missionary. Weekly meetings were held for the women at the packing plant. There was some oposition on the part of Catholics and scoffers. Much visiting was done among Jews and Gentiles, Catholics and Protestants, black folk and white. The Lord moved on the heart of the Greek priest so that he thanked Miss Helgen for doing missionary work among his people and invited her to speak in his church and organize a Sunday-school. He also insisted on her going to another Greek colony to sell Bibles and do personal work. But this priest was too evangelical for the authorities in the church and he soon was hustled out of the city. With the coming of other priests, more self-satisfied, opposition arose among the Greeks.

In 1930 an old six-room house, utterly without conveniences, was rented for mission purposes. Although entirely inadequate for a home and a mission, it seemed to be the best thing at that time. It was purchased and in October of that year Rev. W. B. Olmstead, Missionary Secretary, dedicated it. Two days after Miss Helgen moved into this build-ing she found a note in the door which read: "If you do not get out of here in twenty-four hours we will kill you, you missionary." As soon as Miss Helgen read the note the Lord flooded her mind with His promises. The devil hurt his own cause in this threat, for the news went out in the papers all over the country and many thereby were led to pray for the mission.

Through interested friends the Lord has helped to provide food and clothing for many needy ones. Children's meetings over a period of four years have not been fruitless. Mothers' meetings have been conducted in which lessons in cooking, personal hygiene, care of the child and the sick have been given.

Lehigh is a foreign community at the edge of the city on the northeast. Here iniquity abounds and Catholicism stands like a Gibraltar. When an attempt was made to open a Bible school there a few years ago, the workers were received with the throwing of sticks, tomatoes, eggs and other missiles, and by every kind of noise they knew how to make. Children tried to destroy Miss Helgen's car and anything else they could lay hands on, and watched every opportunity for stealing. Little toddlers used the vilest language. When a worker asked why she was treated so furiously one older child answered with vehemence, "Because you are a Christian, that's why." But the workers succeeded in holding classes forenoons and afternoons for two weeks, and some learned eagerly and rapidly. Now there is a much more friendly spirit at Lehigh. A weekly prayer-meeting is conducted in a Mexican home. When Miss Helgen first began calling she could not find one person who seemed to know anything about the gospel. Now a dear young mother and a lovely young lady, both Greeks, are rejoicing in the Lord. Many Mexicans have prayed and some have been saved. Several joined the Free Methodist Church. Three of these have become active workers.

In these days of depression, anti-foreign sentiment increases in this little city, for the Americans resent the fact that foreigners are holding jobs or getting relief while they are unemployed and needy. While many foreigners are returning to their own lands, many others are here to stay and need the gospel. A recent article in the local newspaper stated that sixty nationalities are represented in Mason City.

Progress in the work has been slow, visible results have been heart-breakingly meager and prospects humanly speaking are none too bright; but many prayers have been heard and answered. He who "takes time off for the funeral of every little gray sparrow" is concerned about these perishing ones from Mexico, Italy, Greece, Poland, Hungary, Bohemia, and other parts of the world. He who can not lie, and whose word shall not return unto Him void, will some day give a bountiful harvest from the seed faithfully sown.

GREEK-AMERICAN MISSION

A Greek-American mission in Chicago, Illinois, started by Mr. George Radeos, was recognized by the Commission on Missions, but with no financial obligation to the Commission. This mission is being carried on with excellent results, and through its radio ministry exerts a wide influence among the Greek people.

CHAPTER IX

THE WOMAN'S MISSIONARY SOCIETY

THE MISSIONARY TIDINGS
MISSIONARY PUBLICATIONS
THE JUNIOR SOCIETY

CHAPTER IX

THE WOMAN'S MISSIONARY SOCIETY

FROM the beginning of Bible history down through the centuries women have had no small part in promoting the interests of the kingdom of God. In New Testament times the women of the early church made a unique contribution to the spread of Christianity.

During the middle ages the women were a great asset in the trying days of the Reformation. Their labors produced results that endured.

The nineteenth century was known as Woman's Century. By the undaunted courage and sublime faith of Mary Lyon a school for the higher education of women was established. And from Mt. Holyoke many young women went out as missionaries to bless the world.

During anti-slavery agitation the most gifted women of the nation joined in the efforts to promote the righteous cause. The strenuous days of the Civil War forced women to organize. They were getting ready for events to follow—the co-operation of church women and the formation of missionary societies.

In the early years of the Free Methodist denomination the women gave strength, poise and stability to the new branch of Methodism.

So far as records show, the first missionary society was organized at Chili Seminary (now A. M.

Chesbrough) in May, 1886. That was the spring following the outgoing and death of Mary E. Carpenter.

Our denominational schools have had a large share in preparing missionaries and have given freely of their energy and support. They deserve our loyal cooperation.

Three years later the first Woman's Foreign Missionary Society was organized at Verona, Pennsylvania, by Mrs. Ella MacGeary in December, 1889. A little later Miss Emma Freeland (Shay) organized at Brooklyn and Utica, New York. She also prepared a tentative Constitution. There was some opposition, but many women joyfully anticipated having a part in this project. Local societies began to multiply. The first conference society was organized in Wisconsin in 1891.

During General Conference at Greenville, Illinois, in 1890 the Committee on Missions added to their report the following recommendation, "That the Missionary Board be authorized to organize a Woman's Foreign Missionary Society, auxiliary to the Board."

From the *General Conference Daily*, October 19, 1894, we glean the following:

This afternoon at two o'clock there will be a meeting of the members of the Woman's Foreign Missionary Societies held in the college chapel. Our object is to form a control organization so as to unify the entire work. Will you come?

On the date of October 23, we read:

The woman's Foreign Missionary Society has perfected its organization, elected its officers, completed a Constitution and By-Laws, and will report to the General Conference through the Committee on Missions.

The committee to draft the Constitution and By-Laws was composed of Mrs. Mary L. Coleman, Mrs. Ella MacGeary and Mrs. Mary L. Stilwell.

The place was Mrs. Stilwell's home on North Locust Street, Greenville.

In the early nineties the sisters in Canada began to form societies. Now there are four well-organized conference societies. Some of our most efficient workers and missionaries hold their citizenship in "The Land of the Maple."

Three years after the formation of the general society, the *Missionary Tidings* was launched. The following year the General Conference voted to give the Woman's Foreign Missionary Society representation on the General Missionary Board and requested that three members be elected at the quadrennial meeting. Mrs. Coleman, Mrs. MacGeary and Mrs. Helen Hart Jones were chosen.

In June, 1903, the quadrennial body was for the first time a delegated body. It was at this time that a Junior Superintendent was elected. At this time an Advisory Board was appointed, and Mrs. Ellen L. Roberts, Mrs. Martha B. Hart and Mrs. Mariet H. Freeland were elected to membership.

It was in 1907 that the first Home Mission Secretary was elected. At that time the work was not under the control of the Missionary Board. It was assumed by the Board in 1921.

The same year, by order of the General Conference, the Executive Committee of the Woman's Foreign Missionary Society was made an advisory board to whom the applications of women candidates should be referred.

At the quadrennial meeting in 1915, the subject of mission study, showing its value and ways of presentation, was clearly set forth. The Executive Committee elected Mrs. Carrie T. Burritt Mission Study Secretary. This task was not given to a general officer until 1931.

In 1919 a separate organization was provided for the young people, as noted elsewhere.

It was in 1923 that the name of the organization was changed from the Woman's Foreign Missionary Society to the Woman's Missionary Society.

It was in 1927 that a time limit for all office-holders was embodied in the Constitution.

In 1931 in the new set-up of church machinery provision was made for two members of the Executive Committee to become members of the Board of Administration.

In each mission field across the sea local Woman's Missionary Societies now exist. The missionaries and native women are carrying on nobly in adapting requirements of the Constitution to their conditions.

The observance of the World Day of Prayer has an important place in our activities.

In the early years it was Mrs. Jensen who, in addition to her duties as treasurer, found time to launch the literature department. Through the years she has watched it grow.

For many years boxes containing an assortment of dried fruits, and other things the missionaries viewed with delight, were sent across the sea. This has required much careful planning and energy on the part of the Box Superintendent. With the exception of a part of one quadrennium when Mrs. Stilwell ably assisted, this task has been performed by a versatile and indefatigable toiler, Mrs. Mary F. Coffee.

To our leaders, elders and pastors the society owes a debt of gratitude for their spirit of brotherly kindness and cooperation. Bishop Roberts favored the organization. It was Bishop Hart who recommended Woman's Foreign Missionary Society representation on the Missionary Board. Bishop Sellew said, "It may well be said of your organization, 'What hath God wrought?' You are a very great asset to the church. No phase of our work has been more signally blessed of God than the efforts of the women in the interests of missions." Rev. J. S. MacGeary said, "Where the missionary society is strongest and most aggressive, there will also be found a spirit of aggressiveness in the work of the church."

To our missionary secretaries who have always evidenced the deepest interest in the work of the society, we are most grateful. The woman who has served so efficiently as office secretary under four of these men—Miss Mabel W. Cook—we highly esteem for her work's sake.

The women who have served as presidents of the general society are:

Ellen Lois Roberts—1894-1903
Mary L. Coleman—1903-1927
Carrie T. Burritt—1927-——

The missionary atmosphere of her uncle's home, her association with the missionaries in the church of her choice, her understanding of human nature, and her life of prayer all contributed to fit Mrs.

Roberts for her duties. It was she who said: "If
you have anything to say, say it strong."

For two score and four years the society was
blessed by the gracious personality of one unusually
gifted in speech and prayer. The ability of Mrs.
Coleman to preside at quadrennial gatherings, and
her knowledge of the fields, was marked.

The forbearance and kindness from a host of loyal
co-workers to her unworthy successor have been
deeply appreciated.

The following list includes the names of the
women who have had a place on the Executive
Committee and the number of years they have
served in one office or another.

Tressa R. Arnold	14	Jenne H. Howland	4
Addie D. Ashcraft	4	Lillian C. Jensen	33
Harriet S. Barnes	9	Helen Hart Jones	8
Adelaide L. Beers	12	Alma L. Miller	7
Agnes Benn	4	Ella L. MacGeary	29
Charlotte T. Bolles	16	Edna C. McCarty	7
Carrie T. Burritt	16	Julia A. Muffitt	20
Adella P. Carpenter	28	Ellen Lois Roberts	9
Jane Coleman	4	Emma Sellew Roberts	13
Mary L. Coleman	37	Mary M. Robinson	16
Ella Maze Daniels	4	Helen I. Root	8
Clara R. Freeland	8	Rebecca E. Sellew	24
Evaline D. Green	4	Emma F. Shay	20
Lillian B. Griffith	12	Alice E. Walls	8
Martha B. Hart	4	Ida C. Winget	16
Emma L. Hogue	20		

Eleven of these have finished their life story. We

EMMA SELLEW ROBERTS

TRESSA R. ARNOLD

REBECCA E. SELLEW

ELLA L. MACGEARY

CHARLOTTE T. BOLLES

MARY M. ROBINSON

CLARA R. FREELAND

EMMA F. SHAY

trust it may be said of each of the thirty-one, "She hath done what she could."

In October, 1934, a brief farewell service was held in behalf of the Woman's Missionary Society rooms at 1134 Washington Boulevard, made sacred by the hallowed presence of the Holy Spirit's visitation. At the new headquarters may He continue to guide.

Statistics for 1934 show: Active members, 11,-657; honorary members, 2.252; *Missionary Tidings* taken, 4,301; receipts of treasurer, $64,124.34. For yearly reports and comparisons consult the *Missionary Tidings* and Conference Minutes.

The success attained has been secured by the faithfulness on the part of individual members in the local societies.

May those who assume the burdens in future years, "Remove not the ancient landmark." May the Master's smile of approval ever rest upon their words and deeds. Our Father, so let it be!

THE MISSIONARY TIDINGS

Intercommunication of religious groups is necessary to their growth and well-being. Our church leaders in early times were men of intelligence and education. Our first bishop, Rev. B. T. Roberts, was conversant with seven languages. Soon after the organization of the church in 1860, he founded a magazine, *The Earnest Christian,* as a medium of communication between the scattered societies. A church paper, *The Free Methodist,* quickly followed in 1868.

The evangelistic spirit of the church prompted

missionaries to go to India, Africa and Japan, and women's societies were formed in the United States and Canada.

What should be done to know of the work of missions in our church? Personal letters and contributions to the *Free Methodist* were highly prized, but were too infrequent and fragmentary to be satisfactory. There was need of some fuller means of communication. Sensing this, Rev. W. T. Hogue, then editor of the *Free Methodist,* later a bishop of the church, issued a "Missionary Supplement" to the paper beginning in May, 1896. He also urged the women of the church to start their own publication.

The first issue of the *Missionary Tidings* was published in January, 1897.

The following women have served as editors:

Mary Weems Chapman—1897-1898
Emma Hillmon Haviland—1898-1899
Emma Sellew Roberts—1899-1907
Tressa Richardson Arnold—1907-1917
Adella P. Carpenter—1917-1931
Helen I. Root—1931- ——

Mrs. Chapman, with her husband, had labored for a time in Liberia, West Africa.

Mrs. Haviland with her husband had served under our board in Portuguese East Africa.

Mrs. Roberts was a sister of Bishop Sellew and joint principal with her husband of the A. M. Chesbrough Seminary. She received much inspiration from the noted India scholar, Pundita Ramabai.

who had brought her daughter and five other girls from India to the school at Chili.

The *Missionary Tidings* continued to grow in favor among the women. The missionaries enriched its pages by contributions.

Under Mrs. Arnold the magazine prospered and was enlarged to twenty-four pages. The departments of Home Missions, Young People and Juniors received due attention. Mrs. Arnold's health failed and she passed away in August, 1917. Of her it may be said, "She hath done what she could."

Miss Carpenter had assumed charge of the literature department in 1916, and the following year was chosen by the Woman's Foreign Missionary Society Executive Committee to serve as editor after the death of Mrs. Arnold.

Again the number of pages was reduced to twenty. In 1919 the Department of Methods was added, with Mrs. Carrie T. Burritt, Mission Study Secretary, in charge.

The Magazine Quiz which had been conducted by Mrs. Burritt was turned over to Mrs. Blanche E. Perigo, who was thus serving at the time of her death in September, 1934.

The Department, "Our Young People," now representing an organization, was headed by its superintendent, Mrs. Hogue, in 1919.

In 1920 the experiment of using a cover for the *Tidings* was tried, but on account of added expense was soon discontinued. The present design of its outside page was furnished by Mrs. Charlotte T. Bolles.

During this period the subscription list reached

its highest point in February, 1924, with a showing of 5,400.

The magazine constantly gives news of the various activities on the foreign and home fields. In Africa it was long a custom to appoint a list of missionaries who, by turn, should write to the *Tidings* each month. Many have proved faithful correspondents.

It is to this magazine our people turn for reports of local, district, conference, and quadrennial gatherings. It is here we find the correct addresses of all missionaries on the field and on furlough.

To meet existing conditions the price of the magazine was changed from fifty cents to sixty-five, then seventy-five, and in 1928 to one dollar. Miss Carpenter gave of her best to promote the interests of the magazine. She served with dignity and grace.

Miss Root, the present editor, had served in Ceylon under the American Board before going to India under our Board. Her work as traveling secretary gave her an insight as to the needs of each section of the country. All this has been an asset in this field of endeavor. During the quadrennium we have had many special numbers.

We deem our magazine worthy to be compared with those of other denominations.

OUR MISSIONARY PUBLICATIONS

G. Harry Agnew, A Pioneer Missionary (317 pages), by Rev. Wilson T. Hogue. A part of the material for this book was written by Mr. Agnew in 1903 while on the African field. He had planned to finish and have it published after his arrival in America, as he and his family were about to sail for home at that time. But before time to sail Mr. Agnew became very ill, and when he realized that death was near he requested his wife, as soon as she reached America, to give what he had prepared to Mr. Hogue and ask him to complete the writing, edit and publish the book for him. Soon after arriving in America, Mrs. Agnew turned over what manuscript she had and assisted Mr. Hogue by giving facts and figures and much valuable information, so that in 1904 the work was completed and the book published.

Missionary Hymns and Responsive Scripture Readings (142 pages) was compiled by Rev. Wilson T. Hogue in 1907, for use in missionary meetings. As soon as the cost of publishing was met by sales, which was less than a year, Mr. Hogue gave the book with copyright to the Woman's Missionary Society. Since then four or five editions, in both cloth and paper covers, have been published.

Clara Leffingwell—A Missionary (320 pages), by Rev. Walter A. Sellew. Published in 1907. This book was written by Mr. Sellew after he had visited our mission field in China. The book not only gives the life story of Miss Leffiingwell, but gives the reader a graphic picture of our mission work in China.

Mariet Hardy Freeland—A Faithful Witness (224 pages). This is the life story of one of the rare mothers of Free Methodism, one who was deeply interested in young people. The author is a daughter, Mrs. Emma Freeland Shay, who has written with deep appreciation of a Christian mother's life and love. This book was written in 1913.

Mary E. Chynoweth—A Missionary (166 pages), by Mrs. Ethel H. Clarke. Miss Chynoweth and Mrs. Clarke were missionaries in India at the time of Miss Chynoweth's death, hence the author could write with sympathy and understanding. This book was published in 1915.

Ellen Lois Roberts—Life and Writings (191 pages), by Miss Adella P. Carpenter. Published in 1926. The author of this valuable book was closely associated with Mrs. Roberts (who was a pioneer mother of Free Methodism) for many years, both in the family and in the A. M. Chesbrough Seminary, of which Bishop Roberts was founder and in which Miss Carpenter was teacher for forty years.

An Alabaster Box—The Life Story of Grace E. Barnes (102 pages), by Miss Helen Isabel Root. Published in 1929. This book, giving the story of a young woman who gave her all to India in loving missionary service, was written by one who herself had served as missionary in India. The work is dedicated to the Young People's Missionary Society of the Free Methodist Church.

India—A Study Book for Juniors, written in 1912 by Mrs. Emma L. Hogue. Five editions published.

Africa—A Study Book for Juniors, by Mrs. Hogue in 1914. Three editions published.

Japan—A Study Book for Juniors, by Mrs. Hogue in 1915. Three editions published.

China—A Study Book for Juniors, by Mrs. Hogue in 1917. Three editions published.

Helps and Hints for Juniors, by Nellie A. Reed.

A Missionary Manual, in 1906, by Mrs. Tressa R. Arnold.

A Guide for Missionary Workers, in 1918, by Mrs. Carrie T. Burritt.

A Sketch of the Woman's Foreign Missionary Society, in 1919, by Mrs. Ella L. MacGeary.

Panama and the Canal Zone, by B. L. Beegle, a missionary to that field. Written especially to furnish material for our missionary societies.

Mexican Missions, by B. H. Pearson, superintendent of our Mexican missions. It is a brief survey of our Home Mission work among the Mexicans in Southern California. Published in 1925.

Our African Work, by Miss Helen Isabel Root. A brief history of the Free Methodist mission work in Africa. Published in 1928.

Glimpses of Victory, by Miss Ruth M. Tapper. Published in 1931. This book gives a brief and comprehensive glimpse of all our mission fields, both home and foreign. This is the first book published as a study book for the Young People's Missionary Society and was written by one of the young people.

For a period of years, helpful and effective calendars, covering the interests and activities of our various fields, were issued.

THE JUNIOR SOCIETY

The record of the early history of the Junior Missionary Society is fragmentary, consisting of mere glimpses of local bands in scattered places where devoted friends of missions realized the need of interesting the children in missions. The story surrounding the first one of which we have a record is full of interest. A dear saint, very ill, and evidently about to cross over to her heavenly home, prayed earnestly that she might live so as to bring up her little family and train them for the Lord. The answer was clear—would she be willing to form a Junior Missionary Society if she were to live? The consecration was made and after her recovery in 1885 she opened her own home for the society. Children came from far and near, some a distance of ten miles. They came that they might receive instruction in sewing, but they received more than that. They worked for Grace Allen in Africa, supported two children in Inhambane, two in South Africa, and gave of their quilts and garments to Olive Branch Mission. The record given of one early year's work surpasses that of many of our good societies of the present time. This was at Gaines, Michigan, and Mrs. Phoebe Proper Stockton was this first "superintendent." It was her lot to share with many others the persecution which came in the early years of missionary organization, and in her case it was the pastor who looked with disfavor

upon what he considered was a questionable innova-
tion. One day he was leading a close class-meeting
and after she had testified he asked what was her
greatest cross. To his surprise she answered hum-
bly, "To follow God in my Junior Missionary work."

A little band who called themselves "The Sunshine
Workers" was organized at Wessington Springs,
South Dakota, by Mrs. Emma F. Shay in 1891. For
some time they did mostly home mission work, holding one foreign meeting a year. Mrs. Ida C. Winget,
superintendent, visited the western coast with her
husband in 1899 and was happy to find a flourishing
society at Seattle, Washington. She tells with what
delight she attended one of their meetings. In 1895
the number of Junior societies had increased suffici-
ently to maintain the support of Miss Nellie Reed,
known as the children's missionary, and this gave
a great impetus to the work.

A study of the growth of the society is an inspiration. There were nineteen societies in 1900. In 1934
there were 533. The 397 members in 1900 were
correspondingly increased to nearly 10,000. During
the seven quadrenniums beginning in 1903 the
money given for missions, in round numbers, has
been $2,000, $5,000, $10,000, $16,000, $27,000,
$27,000, and $29,000 respectively. The high-water
mark for a given year (except membership) was
reached in 1929 when the record shows 530 societies,
10,178 members, and $8,255.63 given for missions.
The present quadrennium has been a testing time
and the figures reflect the difficult years through
which we are passing; and yet through the marvelous

grace of God the work is being carried forward with strength.

In 1907 in order better to describe the character of the growing societies, the name was changed from Junior to Junior and Young People's Societies, this name continuing for twelve years when a separate organization for young people was effected. At this time, Miss Harriet E. Sheldon, newly-elected Superintendent of Juniors, caught the vision of a large unworked field among the babies and small children too young for active membership, and at the following quadrennial meeting provision was made for a Missionary Cradle Roll. This membership, growing steadily from year to year, now numbers 1,969. A larger number, by far, are just outside awaiting but an invitation to be counted in as a part of the Junior family. In 1931 provision was made for Junior-Life membership, and while the years since then have been rather inopportune for many ten-dollar gifts, yet one name after another has been added until they have reached the brave number of sixteen.

The compelling thought in the minds of the early formers of mission bands—the need of missionary instruction—resulted in the publishing of four books, "India," "Africa," "China," and "Japan," written by Mrs. Emma L. Hogue. These excellent little volumes have filled a large place in the missionary education of our Juniors.

Definite objects for giving always have their appeal, and especially so to the mind of the child. Following the support of Nellie Reed was added the support of other missionaries, orphans, scholarships, and various special portions of our missionary work.

The latest project, that of supporting the Junior-age children of our foreign missionaries, has met with a wonderful response. Within a year the support of nearly all has been assumed by the Juniors of the various conferences and this is doubtless a contributing factor in the increased giving of the present year. In reviewing the work of the years, again and again we are led to exclaim, "What hath God wrought!"

The goal: To influence boys and girls to accept Christ as their Savior, and to become enthusiasts for the cause of missions. The motto: "The World Children for Jesus."

The following have served as superintendents:

Ida Collins Winget—1903. Died June 4, 1919.

Harriet Sheldon Barnes—1919-1928.

Edna Crippen McCarty—1928-

CHAPTER X

YOUNG PEOPLE'S MISSIONARY SOCIETY

CHAPTER X

THE YOUNG PEOPLE'S MISSIONARY SOCIETY

1919-1931

THE Young People's Missionary Society was organized at the Quadrennial Meeting held at Greenville, Illinois, in June, 1919.

For several years previous to this time the Executive Committee of the Woman's Foreign Missionary Society (since changed to the Woman's Missionary Society) had seen the need of such an organization, had considered it, but had not felt sure of its feasibility. However, at this session all seemed to realize that the time had come to do something for the young people, who had appealed to them for a separate missionary organization. Accordingly, after much deliberation and prayer, the Young People's Missionary Society was organized and Mrs. Emma L. Hogue was elected superintendent. Her election to this office brought a great burden of responsibility. As wife of a man who had served the church in every office it had to give, from pastor to bishop, she was used to carrying burdens; but to be made responsible for the success or failure of this new society seemed heaviest of all. Then, too, one of the General Conference delegates said to her at this time, "Sister Hogue, you can never put it over. It can't be done." To which she replied, "I know I can't do it, but God can," and He did.

Previous to the organization of the Young People's Missionary Society, the children and young people had carried on their work together as a Junior Missionary Society; but as these boys and girls grew older this was found to be most difficult because of the disparity of ages and interests. As a result we were losing many of our young people to the missionary cause and to the church as well. Many of the young people have testified to this fact, saying, "The Young People's Missionary Society came just in time to save me to the church, for I felt that I must have some real definite work to do for Christ, and I have found it in the Young People's Missionary Society."

It has been a source of joy to Mrs. Hogue that the Young People's Missionary Society was organized while her husband, Bishop Hogue, was living (he passed away eight months later); for at several of the General Conferences he had presented the subject and had urged them to sponsor a Young People's Society, but because some feared that such a society might bring worldliness into the church his efforts failed. Thus he was made happy to know that the young people now had a missionary society of their own. But it was left to the women to give the young people this society.

While we made provision for a separate society for the young people when we organized, yet we had no separate Constitution for them. Therefore, during the first four years we organized local societies only.

As we had no space in our church paper and only

EDNA C. McCARTY

IDA C. WINGET

EVALINE D. GREEN

a page once a month in the *Missionary Tidings,* the superintendent had to do most of the promotional work by personal correspondence, which while very laborious was most enjoyable; for as she said, it was a labor of love—no salary and only the postage.

During this time the conference presidents of the Woman's Missionary Society were asked to get in touch with the district presidents, and they in turn with the local presidents, who had local superintendents elected; and so far as possible a local Young People's Missionary Society in each local church was organized.

As there was no nucleus to start with, we had to feel our way along very carefully; for it was a new and untried field and we must not give offense to those honest ones who did not yet favor the new organization. But the God of missions smiled upon the new society from the first, and His blessing rested upon the work. During the first four months these local societies raised and sent into the missionary treasury $646.83. At the close of the first quadrennium we reported 200 local societies, a membership of 3,208, and $12,000 raised. Besides this, the societies contributed considerable money for special purposes.

How happy these young people were in their work in mission study, Bible study, holding missionary meetings and entering every open door of service.

But youth is aggressive, and now they were asking for broader fields of activity. They wanted district and conference societies and were looking to their mother society to provide them. Members of the W. M. S. and some of the brethren also saw this need. Accordingly, the matter was brought before the Executive Committee at their October meeting in 1922. It never will be known how much the Young People's Missionary Society owe to Mrs. Mary L. Coleman, who was then president of the Woman's Missionary Society, and to other members of the committee, for their sympathy and cooperation in planning and providing for a better working equipment for their society. A committee of five was appointed at this meeting to prepare a tentative Constitution and By-Laws for young people's societies, with a larger committee for consultation by correspondence, representing all sections of the Woman's Missionary Society. This tentative Constitution was presented to the quadrennial meeting held at Corunna, Michigan, the following year, June, 1923. After careful consideration and several changes, this Constitution and By-Laws was completed and adopted by that body. A handbook also was ordered to be prepared, and was later adopted and ordered bound with the Constitution and By-Laws. This Constitution, with a few changes and additions, was used by the Young People's Missionary Society during the twelve years that it was auxiliary to the Woman's Missionary Society.

In this meeting at Corunna an effort was made by some of the General Conference members to have a Young People's Society to supplant the Young People's Missionary Society; but this plan did not meet with approval and so the Young People's Missionary Society was left free to go on with its work for the next four years.

The first Constitution of the Young People's Missionary Society gives as the object of the society the following:

1. To seek and maintain among its members the highest type of Christian experience and life, through the regeneration and the baptism of the Holy Spirit.

2. To interest, train, and enlist the young people in the evangelization of the world field, both at home and abroad.

3. To study the needs of the various fields and become intelligent supporters of the full missionary program.

4. To raise money for objects sanctioned by the general authorities of the church and in ways thoroughly in accord with its Discipline.

The payment of one dollar a year entitled one to membership, and payment of $15.00 constituted life membership. All young people of good moral character, fourteen years of age or over, could become members of the society.

Some good people were opposed to taking those into the society who were not professed Christians; but the majority felt that such action would hinder the work of the society. Besides, we had these safeguards in the Constitution: "In the local society, the president of the Woman's Missionary Society and the pastor shall be members of the executive committee. The local president shall be a member of the Free Methodist Church, and whenever practicable the other local officers. The district and conference officers shall be members of the Free Methodist Church."

At the time when this matter was under discussion, Bishop Clark said to the superintendent: "A missionary society would not be an attractive place for worldly-minded young people. They either will become Christians or soon drop out." Many of those who were unconverted when they joined the society became active and devoted Christians.

Within three months after our Constitution was sent out fifteen conferences reported that they had organized. Southern California was the first, Oregon the second. So the work grew and increased rapidly. And yet there were some pastors and members who still were opposed to local, district and conference societies. This was very discouraging to the young people who were involved; but they were advised by their superintendent to wait on the Lord, be patient, never to show a bad spirit or try to force the issue, respect the wishes of their pastor and members, and God would give them the desires of their heart. This invariably proved true.

The first Young People's Missionary Society Summer Conference was held on the camp ground in Glen Ellyn, Illinois, July 6-8, 1926. The Illinois, Indiana, Iowa, Michigan and Wisconsin conferences cooperated in this meeting. Courses in Bible Study, Home and Foreign Missions, Normal Methods, Story-Telling and Song-Leadership were given. In the evening they had talks by missionaries and an evangelistic sermon. The Chicago District sponsored the meeting, and Mrs. Lillian B. Griffith, who was district superintendent at the time, worked faithfully to make the meeting a success. Rev. W. J. Bone, district elder, and Mrs. Emma L. Hogue, general superintendent, were the Executive Committee of the Chicago District and assisted in the work. Mrs. Evaline D. Green, Mrs. Rachel Ghormley and Mrs. Emma Stoll from McPherson, Kansas, were invited help, and by their teaching and speaking added much to the interest of the meeting. The Morning Watch from 6 to 6:30 each day and the Good-Night Prayer services were times of special blessings. God's approval rested upon this, our first Summer Conference, and a number of young people were saved and sanctified and the Young People's Missionary Society work in the conferences represented was advanced.

During this second quadrennium the Young People's Missionary Society held many local institutes, district and conference conventions, a number of which the General Superintendent attended, traveling 5,000 miles during the quadrennium. She visited the Washington and Oregon Conferences, some in the midwest and some in the east, nine altogether, visiting and speaking in many of the locals. Visiting these parts of the work was a source of encouragement and delight, and helped her to see the needs, also to realize what capable and Spirit-filled young people made up the Young People's Missionary Society. These societies were holding mission study classes, Bible study classes, reading campaigns and contests; were visiting the sick and shut-ins; holding meetings in jails and on the streets, and assisting the pastor as he called upon them. One pastor reported that whenever he had to be away on a Sunday evening he did not send away for a speaker, but left the service in the hands of the Young People's Missionary Society, and they always proved equal to the occasion. Besides these activities, many of the societies made supplies and sent to the hospitals and to the missionaries on the home and foreign fields. Nine conferences were publishing their own papers.

At the close of this quadrennium there were thirty-seven conference societies, 330 local societies —an increase of 130—and a membership of 6,208 —an increase of 3,000. They had raised $56,678.99, an increase of $45,287.37 over the previous quadrennium. During the last year of the quadrennium they raised $21,808.87, enough to pay the salaries of forty missionaries on the field. Best of all, a large number of the young people were led to accept Christ as their Savior, and others were brought into a closer relation to Him.

However, the Young People's Missionary Society did not have easy sailing during all of these four years. Opposition fierce and strong was encountered from some who still wanted a regular church society, with perhaps a missionary department instead of a Young People's Missionary Society. As a result of this situation, the Woman's Missionary Society knew that in order to have peace in their borders there must be some changes and adjustments made at the next quadrennial meeting.

Then there had been a lack of cooperation of the Woman's Missionary Society in some places, as they felt that the Young People's Missionary Society kept the young people from coming into the Woman's Missionary Society and strengthening it. No doubt a large part of this trouble might have been lessened if the young women had joined the

Woman's Missionary Society when they reached the age of twenty-five or thirty at the latest. Perhaps if the Woman's Missionary Society had laid plans to use these young people in greater activities than were usually carried on in their society they might have done this. These young people had been used to doing things in their Young People's Missionary Society and were loath to become less active. Yet in spite of some rough sailing (which helps to make strong sailors) the Young People's Missionary Society made unlooked for progress in numbers, in money raised, in missionary activities, and in spiritual growth during the quadrennium.

In June, 1927, the quadrennial meeting was held at Rochester, New York. As one entered the assembly room one of the first things to attract attention was the very fine exhibit prepared by the Young People's Missionary Society from all parts of the United States and Canada. There were unusually suggestive posters and pennants, and the made-up books on the Young People's Missionary Society study book—"Young Islam on Trek"—were works of art. All who saw them said that in originality, suggestiveness and execution they were the finest they had ever seen.

At this quadrennial session there were a number of interested young people present, but they had no part in the deliberations of the body. This was unfortunate, and the matter having been presented by the General Superintendent, the body gladly voted to give the Young People's Missionary Society representation at their next quadrennial meeting. This action was greatly appreciated by the young people.

At this session the General Conference, which was meeting at the same time, voted its approval of a Young People's Society to be under the control of the church, but in no way to do away with or take the place of the Young People's Missionary Society, which was to remain auxiliary to the Woman's Missionary Society. In the interest of peace the majority of the quadrennial members voted favorably to having this new society. From this time the Young People's Missionary Society was to confine itself to missionary activities only, leaving the new society to carry on various lines of work formerly a part of and carried on by the Young People's Missionary Society. So the quadrennium began with two young people's societies. Would this work well? Some had their doubts. Any local church could have and was urged to have the two societies.

A Young People's Council was elected, composed of seven members, two of whom—the president of the Woman's Missionary Society and the superintendent of the Young People's Missionary Society —were members. During the second year after Mrs. Hogue's election as superintendent, the Executive Committee of the Woman's Missionary Society elected her assistant to Miss Adella P. Carpenter in her work as Literature Agent. Mrs. Hogue gave only part time to this work, and as she was paid by the hour could give necessary time to the Young People's Missionary Society. Being in the Publishing House office (our Literature Department is in that building) she could help select and send out suitable books, leaflets and helps for use of the Young People's Missionary Societies. This part of the work Miss Carpenter gave her to do. She continued in this position for seven years.

At this quadrennial meeting, when the Executive Committee urged her to take the work of Literature Agent (Miss Carpenter not wishing to continue in the office), she had a conviction that she should give her individual time to the Young People's Missionary Society. But the question of support was raised. She had never had a salary as superintendent, did not wish any, and up to this time had received only fifty dollars a year for promotional work, postage, typing, etc. This amount was paid by the Woman's Missionary Society from their Contingent Fund, thus leaving all funds raised by the Young People's Missionary Society to go into the missionary treasury. As Mrs. Hogue felt that this was the Lord's leading, she left the office in Chicago and went to live with her daughter and family in Springfield, Illinois. However, she spent most of her time during the last four years traveling in the interests of the Young People's Missionary Society. When not raised on the field, her traveling expenses were provided for from the Contingent Fund of the Woman's Missionary Society.

During this quadrennium plans were worked out for representation of the Young People's Missionary Society at the next quadrennial meeting of the Woman's Missionary Society. The Woman's Missionary Society voted that twenty-five cents a member should be raised during the quadrennium to meet the expenses of the delegates. Then it was voted that all conferences having an active membership of 300 or more should be entitled to a delegate, and the other conferences should be grouped to make the 300 membership. This grouping was rather difficult, but the results were quite satisfactory. Eight conferences had the 300 members—East Michigan, Genesee, Illinois, Oil City, Pittsburgh, Southern California, Wabash, Washington. As there were eleven groups, the Young People's Missionary Society was entitled to nineteen delegates. These delegates and reserve delegates were to be elected at the last annual conference Young People's Missionary Society meeting before the quadrennial meeting. Each delegate representing a group was requested to consult each of the other delegates in the group, getting his views and wishes as to what should be done at this meeting in order to best promote and conserve the work, and at the close these delegates also were to report the meeting to the other conferences.

An interesting program was prepared and printed for the Young People's Missionary Society meeting.

At the quadrennial meeting held at Greenville, Illinois, June 11-22, 1931, eighteen of the nineteen Young People's Missionary Society delegates met with the Woman's Missionary Society in their first sitting. What an inspiration this first meeting together was to both groups. At this time the Young People's Missionary Society delegates presented their credentials and the General Superintendent introduced them by name to the body.

In the afternoon the Young People's Missionary Society delegates met together for their first regular sitting in the large, pleasant room in the basement of the Free Methodist Church. The exhibit which met the eye on entering the room was a rare treat.

There were posters, mottoes, maps, etc., which literally covered the walls. Then there were seventeen lovely quilts, booklets, curios, bandages, pillows, scrap-books, etc., etc. Several conferences had made booklets telling the history of their Young People's Missionary Society, with pictures of various officers. The West Ontario Young People's Missionary Society had a large map made on muslin showing the location of their different locals. China contributed three most wonderful maps—one of China, one of the Eastern continent and one of the Western, hand-made by Chinese young women. At the close of the session prizes were awarded the best by the superintendent. Oil City Conference showed 151 pieces and took the first prize of $10.00. Wabash took second prize, $5.00, and Ohio third of $3.00, which were paid personally by Mrs. Hogue.

At the first sitting after a devotional period the Young People's Missionary Society body organized by the election of officers as follows: President, Rev. Harold Ryckman of the Southern California Conference; secretary, Rev. Thurber Thayer of the Genesee Conference; treasurer, Rev. Harry Webb of the Ohio Conference; reporter, Paul N. Ellis of the Wabash Conference. At this sitting Miss Adella P. Carpenter presented to the society an ink-well which had been used by Bishop B. T. Roberts, founder of our church. Miss Carpenter made the presentation with these words, "This means that you are to use your pens for God," to which eighteen young hearts responded, "I will."

Business and program sittings were held each morning and afternoon. A study of our mission fields was conducted each day by Miss Ruth Tapper of the Illinois Conference. All delegates reported the work of their conferences, including those of the groups they represented. Short talks on ways and means of increasing interest in their meetings, of being more competent officers, and of making their work more spiritual and effective were given by the delegates. Each day a talk was given by a missionary on furlough. One afternoon the Greenville Young People's Missionary Society entertained the visiting young people at a campus reception. This spirit of hospitality shown by the local society made the delegates feel acquainted and more at home during the session. As Mr. Ellis reported: "In all our sittings the Holy Spirit was manifest in our devotions. Several times during the meetings our president made a special call to prayer, and God was present in a remarkable way."

One whole day of this session was given to a joint meeting of the Woman's Missionary Society and the Young People's Missionary Society, Mrs. Hogue, superintendent, in charge. Mrs. Burritt, president of the Woman's Missionary Society, gave an address of welcome to the young people. Among other things she said, "You are an asset, not a problem." Mr. Ellis from the Wabash Conference responded. Many fine addresses were given by both young people and older ones, and these were interspersed with quartets and special songs by the young people. Several of them spoke on "What the Young People's Missionary Society Has Meant in My Life." The whole day was just packed full of good, helpful, inspirational and spiritual food for old and young. At this joint meeting the Young People's Missionary Society brought a unanimous petition to the Woman's Missionary Society, asking that an exception to the twelve-year limit for general conference officers be made that their superintendent (who had served twelve years) might continue in office another four years. As it was not thought best to make any exceptions to the rule, the Young People's Missionary Society later nominated Mrs. Lillian B. Griffith for the place.

You will remember that we started out our quadrennium in 1927 with two young people's societies in the field, the Young People's Missionary Society, which had been operating as auxiliary to the Woman's Missionary Society for eight years, and the Young People's Society, just organized as a church society.

Although it was quite difficult sometimes to carry on two young people's organizations in so small a church, yet as a Young People's Missionary Society we succeeded remarkably well. Contrary to the prophecy of some, who said that with the two societies the Young People's Missionary Society would come up at the next quadrennium with a loss, the society grew and prospered as never before. The superintendent spent her time in building up and helping and encouraging the young people in their work. She was in the East and West, traveling over 12,000 miles the last year.

At the end of twelve years we had forty-two conference organizations, 433 societies and 7,180 members. The members of the Young People's Missionary Society are largely tithers, which accounts for their fine contribution of $104,080.33 to our mission fund during the last quadrennium. This large amount made all very happy.

The activities of the Young People's Missionary Society had been many and varied and had greatly increased during the quadrennium. Besides their former activities, they held Bible Study and Holiness Conventions, with gracious results in the salvation of souls. The Stewardship Pledges were signed by thousands. Mrs. Griffith helped much in the organization of conference societies as she visited these conferences with her husband, Bishop Griffith.

The Young People's Missionary Society distributed thousands of tracts and Scripture portions in both English and foreign languages. They have the missionary vision and realize that a missionary must be a soul-winner. They have accepted the missionary challenge, "Go ye into all the world, and preach the gospel to every creature," and are gladly responding, "Here am I, Lord, send me." Their motto given them in the beginning is "Others."

However, in some places there was considerable friction over the two societies, caused partly by lack of wisdom and perhaps of grace; but through it all the Woman's Missionary Society did not enter into the controversy but carried on the work of the Young People's Missionary Society as before. In the meantime, the Young People's Society was not gaining ground very fast, and some of its promoters urged the Woman's Missionary Society to turn over the Young People's Missionary Society to the church with the removal of the "M," thus doing away with the missionary society. This the Woman's Missionary Society felt not best to do; for the Young People's Missionary Society was the connecting link between the Juniors and the Woman's Missionary Society. Besides, the Young People's Missionary Society was a vine of God's own planting and must not be destroyed. Neither did the majority of the young people want the "M" removed, for they were thoroughly missionary in spirit and in labors. The following was written by a young man, president of a conference Young People's Missionary Society:

When we take the "M" from Y. P. M. S we will become a society with young people but without that burning interest in the promotion of Christ's kingdom. At present the Young People's Missionary Society is a great organization with a great purpose. Why not look at the young people's societies of other churches? Young people must be tied to a great purpose to accomplish a great work. Young people can receive no greater challenge to serve than that found in working toward the upbuilding of the kingdom through the development of a real missionary zeal.

At this time both the Woman's Missionary Society and the General Conference had come to feel that there should be but one society for the young people in order to have harmony and union of spirit and effort and to save the young people to God and the church. But how was this to be done? There was much consideration and prayer given to the matter in the Young People's Missionary Society committee and in the general body of the Woman's Missionary Society. Finally the Committee on Young People from the church and the Committee on Young People's Missionary Society from the Woman's Missionary Society held long sittings together and worked out what proved to be an acceptable solution of the problem. This report was accepted by the Woman's Missionary Society and adopted as a whole. It was also presented to the General Conference, and stated that it already had been approved by the General Woman's Missionary Society. The General Conference adopted the report wihout changing a word. A few voted against it.

Now the Young People's Missionary Society is a church society and yet is a missionary society and vitally connected with the Woman's Missionary Society. The Woman's Missionary Society feel that there is no real loss but gain in having this society transferred to the control of the Free Methodist Church, while it still remains a connecting link between the Juniors and the Woman's Missionary Society in their missionary program. As Miss Root, editor, reported in the *Missionary Tidings*: "The new quadrennium begins in an atmosphere of eager hope and faith." Before the adoption of the paper, Mrs. Lillian B. Griffith had been nominated superintendent by the Young People's Missionary Society and elected by the Woman's Missionary Society. In accordance with provisions of the new plan she also was nominated and elected by the General Conference.

It is significant that the Young People's Missionary Society should have had its birth in Greenville and at the same place after twelve years of most successful missionary service should pass with the

EMMA L. HOGUE

MRS. LILLIAN B. GRIFFITH

ELLA MAZE DANIELS

LILLIAN CAMP JENSEN

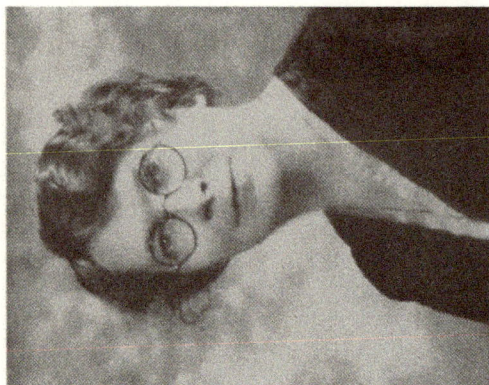

JENNE HARROUN HOWLAND

ALICE E. WALLS

"M" in under the control of the church to which we all have sworn allegiance. Quoting again from the *Missionary Tidings*: "So much for what was done. But how? That is another story. In it are included days and nights of prayer, determined waiting till the right hour for action struck, not controversy, not scheming, just straightforward thinking and that waiting, waiting till the Holy Spirit actually brought opinions apparently irreconcilable into real harmony. To Him be heartfelt praise!"

And now at the close of twelve years we erect our Ebenezer, "our stone of help," our monument of gratitude and praise. Let us tell to all the world, "Hitherto hath the Lord helped us." The word "hitherto" means more than it says—it carries henceforward wrapped up in it. He has helped. He will help. So with God's blessing and the baptism of the Holy Spirit may the Young People's Missionary Society heed God's command to "Go forward."

YOUNG PEOPLE'S MISSIONARY SOCIETY

1931-1935

The General Conference of 1931 merged the two young people's organizations—the Young People's Society and the Young People's Missionary Society—into one church young people's society, the Young People's Missionary Society. A new chapter was added to the Discipline, providing for a close tie-up between the Young People's Missionary Society and the church. The local, district, conference and general superintendents are elected by the church and responsible to the church. The pastors and district elders are members of the respective executive boards.

The superintendents of the Young People's Missionary Society, however, are members of the Woman's Missionary Society and may be nominated by the Woman's Missionary Society; and the superintendents and the presidents of the Woman's Missionary Society are members of the respective executive boards of the Young People's Missionary Society. The superintendents also continue as members of the Woman's Missionary Society executive committees. The Commission on Missions and five members of the Woman's Missionary Society Executive Committee constitute the general Young People's Missionary Society Council.

The Discipline provides further that the Young People's Missionary Society shall be distinctly missionary in aim and motive, that there shall be twelve missionary meetings during the year, with one rally at which time an offering and subscriptions shall be taken for missions, and that all mission money shall be used only for objects included in the appropriations of the Commission on Missions.

Christ's worldwide program was gladly accepted by the young people as their platform. His ways of carrying out His plan, through service, through teaching or education, through stewardship, through evangelism and all through the Holy Spirit, were also gladly accepted and practiced. As the colors of the rainbow all unite to make one primary color, so the varied Young People's Missionary Society activities, studies, services, meetings, departments, all unite to make Christ known. This goal, to make Christ known, so challenged all groups that the slogan, "United to Make Christ Known," was unanimously accepted.

Through the Sunday evening services held in the main room of the church open to all, the adult membership of the church has come to a fuller understanding of the great worthwhile objectives of the Young People's Missionary Society, and hence to a fuller cooperation with the young people in their world task.

The through-the-week activities have challenged the young people by giving to each the glory of a definite task on which he works throughout the year and on which he reports regularly to his department head, and by bringing them together often for purposes in harmony with their motto, "Others," and their slogan, "United to Make Christ Known." Meetings to practice and memorize the old hymns; to clip and file facts, pictures and stories for use on bulletin boards and in programs; to clean, repair, press and pack garments for Christ's needy ones; to make posters and scrap-books—have brought the joy of fellowship with each other, but far more—the joy of fellowship with Him in His care for "Others."

The growth of the organization during the quadrennium is reflected in a comparison of the first report in 1931 and the 1934 report. The gains in each item are as follows:

Local societies, 145; active members, 3,336; honorary members, 829; missionary meetings with offerings, 2,602; weekly Sunday services with subjects as given in the *Free Methodist,* 6,615; societies practicing the Thank-Offering, 165; societies practicing the Penny-a-Day self-denial, 252; books read, 14,450; reading campaigns, 223; Christian education meetings with offerings, 326; used garments, 4,297; new supplies, $613.54; new signers of Stewardship Pledge, 2,529; stewardship meetings, 1,110; pre-service prayer-meetings, 2,300; prayer circles, 184; quiet hour comrades, 829; tracts distributed, 110,217; Gospels, 1,953; visits, 19,719; cottage and institutional prayer-meetings, 1,831; societies observing Pre-Easter Evangelism, 84; Sunday-schools organized, 24; conversions, 926; accessions to the church, 1,041; Y. P. M. S. Reading Course Certificates, 17; standard societies, 15; missionary money, $2,272.85.

The Young People's Missionary Society Council during this period has provided a suggestive program for each Sunday evening service, on the required subjects; has issued an undated series of suggestive outlines in pamphlet form which has been well received throughout the constituency, and tens of thousands of leaflets on the various activities; has published a mission study book for use by our Young People's Missionary Society, "Glimpses of Victory," from our own fields; and has in preparation now another mission study book on "The Lives of Our Missionaries."

The regional conferences, instituted the first year of the quadrennium, have been a great source of instruction and inspiration to the young people.

The Young People's Missionary Society during

1934, the peak of the depression, raised more than enough missionary money to support all of our missionaries, home and foreign.

The Young People's Missionary Society has been happy in its place as a part of the Free Methodist Church and its members have been glad to serve in every department of the church—regular church services, Sunday-school, class-meetings, prayer-meetings, junior work, our schools, and our Woman's Missionary Society, as well as through their own Young People's Missionary Society. The reciprocity that has resulted because of these inter-relationships between the various departments of the church and the Young People's Missionary Society is beautiful to see.

What the Motto, "The Evangelization of the World in This Generation," was to a former generation of Christian youth our Young People's Missionary Society slogan, "United to Make Christ Known," has been to our Free Methodist youth.

www.ingramcontent.com/pod-product-compliance
Lightning Source LLC
Chambersburg PA
CBHW031952040426
42448CB00006B/324

* 9 7 8 1 6 2 1 7 1 4 9 3 4 *